Thomas Talmage

The Palestine Sermons

Thomas Talmage

The Palestine Sermons

ISBN/EAN: 9783337294014

Printed in Europe, USA, Canada, Australia, Japan

Cover: Foto ©Lupo / pixelio.de

More available books at **www.hansebooks.com**

THE
PALESTINE SERMONS
OF
REV. T. DE WITT TALMAGE, D. D.
DELIVERED DURING HIS TOUR OF
THE ∴ HOLY ∴ LAND.
FOR HIS MILLIONS OF READERS AT
HOME AND ABROAD,

INCLUDING GRAPHIC DESCRIPTIONS OF SACRED PLACES;
VIVID DELINEATIONS OF GOSPEL TRUTHS; INTERESTING LOCAL REMINISCENCES; AND VARIED
MISCELLANY, AS INSPIRED BY

HIS VISIT TO THE MANY PLACES MADE SACRED BY THE
PERSONAL PRESENCE OF JESUS CHRIST AND THE
GREAT HOST OF BIBLICAL CHARACTERS.

"Talk about questions of the day, there is but one question, and that is the Gospel. It can and will correct everything needing correction."—GLADSTONE'S REMARK TO DR. TALMAGE AT HAWARDEN.

ILLUSTRATED.

COPYRIGHT 1890.
CHICAGO:
RHODES & McCLURE PUBLISHING (
1890.

CONSTANTINOPLE, January, 1890.

On leaving America I addressed some words of farewell to my sermonic readers, and now, on my way home, I will write this letter of salution which will probably reach you about the Monday that will find me on the Atlantic ocean, from which I cannot reach you with the usual sermon. I have completed the journey of inspection for which I came. Others may write a life of Christ without seeing the Holy Land. I did not feel conpetent for such a work until I had seen with my own eyes the sacred places, and so I left home and church and native country for a more arduous undertaking. I have visited all the scenery connected with our Lord's history. The whole journey has been to me a surprise, an amazement, a grand rapture or a deep solemity. I have already sent to America my Holy Land observations for my Life of Christ, and they were written on horseback, on muleback, on camelback, on ship's deck, by dim candle in tent, in mud hovel of Arab village, amid the ruins of old cities, on Mount of Beatitudes, on beach of Genesareth, but it will take twenty years of sermons to tell what I have seen and felt on this journey through Palestine and Syria.

All things have combined to make our tour instructive and advantageous. The Atlantic, and Mediterranean, and Adriatic, Ægean, Dardanelles, and Marmora seas have treated us well. Since we left New York we have had but a half day and one night of storm, and that while crossing Mount Hermon. But let only those in robust health attempt to go the length of Palestine and Syria on horseback. I do not think it is because of the unhealthiness of climate in the Holy Land that so many have sickened and died here or afterward as a result of visiting these lands, but because of the fatigue of travel. The number of miles gives no indication of the exhaustion of the way. A hundred and fifty miles in Palestine and Syria on horseback demand as much physical strength as four hundred miles on horseback in regions of easy journey.

Because of the near two months of bright sunlight by day and bright moonlight or starlight by night, the half day of storm was to us the more memorable. It was about noon of Dec. 18, that the tempest struck us and drenched the mountains. One of the horses falls and we halt amid a blinding rain. It is freezing cold. Fingers and feet like ice. Two hours and three-quarters before encampment. We ride on in silence, longing for the terminus of to-day's pilgrimage. It is, through the awful inclemency of the weather, the only dangerous day of the journey. Slip and slide and stumble and climb and descend we must, sometimes on the horse and sometimes off, until at last we halt in the hovel of a village, and instead of entering camp for the night we are glad to find this retreat from the storm. It is a house of one story, built out of mud. My room is covered with a roof of goats' hair. A feeble fire mid-floor, but no chimney. It is the best house of the village. Arabs, young and old, stand around in wonderment as to why we come. There is no window in the room, but two little openings, one over the door, the other in the wall, through which latter opening I occasionally find an Arab face thrust to see how I am progressing. But the door is open, so I have some light.

This is an afternoon and night never to be forgotten for its exposures and acquaintance with the hardships of what an Arab considers luxurious apartment. I sat that night by a fire the smoke of which finding no appropriate place of exit took lodgement in my nostrils and eyes. For the first time in my life I realized that chimnies were luxury, but not a necessity. The only adornments in this room were representations of two tree branches in the mud of the wall, a circle supposed to mean a star, a bottle hung from the ceiling, and about twelve indentations in the wall to be used as mantels for anything that may be placed there. This storm was not a surprise. Though pessimistic prophets we had expected that at this season we should have rain and snow and hail throughout our journey. For the most part it has been sunshine and tonic atmosphere, and not a moment has our journey been hindered. Gratitude to God is with us the dominant emotion.

Having visited the scenery connected with Christ's life, I was glad to close my journey by passing through the apostolic lands and seas. You can hardly imagine our feelings as we came in sight of Damascus, and on the very road where Saul was unhorsed at the flash of the supernal light. We did not want, like him, to be flung on the earth, but we did hope for some great spiritual blessing, brighter than any noonday sun, and a new preparation for usefulness. Our long horseback ride was ended, for a carriage met us some miles out and took us back to the city. The impression one receives as he rides along the walled gardens of the place are different from those produced by any other city.

But we cannot describe our feelings as we entered the city about which we have heard and read so much, the oldest city under the sun, and founded by the grandson of Noah; nor our emotions as we pass through the street called "Straight," along which good Ananias went to meet Saul. and by the site of the palace of Naaman, the leper, and saw the river Abana, as yesterday we saw Pharpar, the rivers of Damascus that Naaman preferred to wash in rather than the Jordan. Strange and unique Damascus! It is worth while to cross the Atlantic and Europe to see it. Though it has been the place of battle and massacre, and of ancient affluence and splendor as well as it is of present prosperity, to me its chief attraction arises from the fact that here the scales fell from Paul's eyes, and that chief of apostles here began that mission which will not end until heaven is peopled with ransomed spirits. So also I saw day before yesterday Patmos, where John heard the trumpets, and the waves of the sea dashed to his feet, reminding him of the songs of heaven, "like the voice of many waters."

But this letter can only give a hint of the things we mean to tell you about when we get home, where we expect to be before this month is ended. I baptized by immersion in the Jordan an American whom we met, and who desired the solemn ordinance administered to him in the sacred waters.

I rolled down from Mount Calvary or "place of a skull" a stone for the corner stone of our new Brooklyn Tabernacle.

We bathed in the "Dead Sea" and in "Gideon's Fountain," where his three hundred men eagerly lapped the water from their hands as they passed through; and we sailed on Lake Galilee and stood on Mount Zion, and Mount Moriah, and Mount Hermon, and I saw the place where the shepherds heard the Christmas anthem the night Christ was born: and have been at Nazareth, and Capernaum, and sat by "Jacob's Well," and saw Tele-el-Kebir of modern battle, and Megiddo of ancient battle, and where the Israelites crossed the desert, and slept at Bethel where one ladder was let down into Jacob's dream, but the night I slept there the heavens were full of ladders, first a ladder of clouds, then a ladder of stars, and all up and down the heavens were the angels of beauty, angels of consolation, angels of God ascending and descending; and I was on nearly all the fields of Herodic, and Solomonic, and Davidic, and Abrahamic history.

I took Rome and Naples and Athens, and Alexandria and Cairo on the way out, and take the Greek Archipelago, and Constantinople, and Vienna on the way back. What more can God in his goodness grant me in the way of natural scenery, and classic association, and spiritual opportunity? Ah yes! I can think of something gladder than that he can grant me. Safe return to the people of my beloved flock, the field of my work, and the land where my father died, and in the dust of whose valley I pray God I may be buried.

T. DE WITT TALMAGE.

Hon. William E. Gladstone.

DR. TALMAGE'S CALL ON MR. GLADSTONE.

"Pray come to Hawarden to-morrow," telegraphed Mr. Gladstone to Dr. Talmage, Jan. 23, 1890. The invitation was gladly accepted, and the reception given by the Ex Premier was very cordial. The two gentlemen had a long talk on religious and political questions. Mr. Gladstone said:

"Talk about the questions of the day, there is but one question, and that is the Gospel. It can and will correct everything needing correction. All men at the head of great movements are Christian men. During the many years I was in the Cabinet I was brought into association with sixty master minds and all but five of them were Christians. My only hope for the world is in bringing the human mind into contact with divine revelation." Then placing his hand on Dr. Talmage's shoulder, Mr. Gladstone warmly eulogized the doctor's

Christian zeal and expressed his great gratification at the marvelous publicity given to his sermons, which are now distributed in all lands and read in all languages.

After luncheon the two men linked arms and took a walk over Mr. Gladstone's vast estate, its proprietor commenting lovingly on its wonderful trees as though they were human beings. He then inquired eagerly if Americans paid proper attention to tree culture. Dr. Talmage asked Mr. Gladstone if the Irish home rule would be victorious. Gladstone brightened up and responded emphatically; "Yes when next election comes." He continued: "It seems to be a dispensation of God that I should be engaged in battle. At my time of life I should be resting. I never had any option in these matters. I dislike contests, but when Ireland, once the refuge of persecuted Englishmen, showed herself ready to adopt a righteous constitution and do her full duty, I hesitated not a moment to espouse her cause."

Concerning America he said: "No one outside of the United States is bound to love it more than I." Pointing to the numerous beautiful gifts from America he went on to say: "Everywhere I have practical expression of the tender thoughtfulness and kindness of the American people."

Toward evening, when bidding Dr. Talmage farewell, Mr. Gladstone pressed into his hands some books and pamphlets containing autographic inscriptions, and also a copy of his own Latin rendering of his favorite hymn, "Rock of Ages," and said: "Give my highest regards to President Harrison and express to Mr. Blaine my deepest sympathy with him on account of the loss of his beloved son."

CONTENTS.

"LIFE'S GREAT VOYAGE:" 17
Off for the Holy Land, 17
Paul as a Sailor, 18
Ancient Navigation, 19
Trampling the Billows, 20
The Church is the Dry Dock, 22
Love is the Helm, 22
Hope is the Anchor, 23
Faith is our Canvas' 23
Prayer is the Rigging, 24
The Bible is the Compass, 24
Look out for Icebergs, 25
Keep your Colors Up, 25
Christ is the Pilot, 26
Incidents, 26
Once More I Confess My Faith, 28
Good By. 29

"A MEDITERRANEAN VOYAGE:" 31
The Appian Way, 31
Paul as a Signal Officer, 32
An Excited Crew, 33
An Awful Shipwreck, 33
Tempters Are Not Helpers, 35
Dangerous to Refuse Good Advice, 36
In a Cyclone on the Sea, 38
We Expected to Die, 39
The Terrified Passengers, 40
Wild Cry of the Cyclone, 41
My Dying Prayer, 42
The Beautiful Morning, 43
The Glorified Shore, 45

"THE CLOUDED VISION:" 47
The Illustrious Paul, 47
The Splendor of Ancient Corinth, 48
Paul Addressed the Highest Culture, 49
Our Dim Vision Will Grow Brighter, 50
This is True of our Knowledge of God, 50
And True of the Saviour's Excellency, 51

God's Providences Not Fully Understood, 54
Providential Hindrances in Life, 55
How Many Shall Be Saved? 56
A Glorious and Everlasting Reunion, 58

"THE BELOVED DORCAS." 61
Dorcas and Napoleon, 61
An Eloquent Tribute, 62
Great Weeping in Joppa, 63
The Apostle Peter Appears on the Scene, 63
Dorcas the Disciple, 64
Dorcas the Benefactress, 66
Queen Blanche and Queen Maud, 68
Burial of Josephine of France, 70
A Story of the Queen of England. 73

"THE GOLDEN AGE of JERUSALEM'" 75
Jerusalem!—Its Mighty Past, 75
Solomon's Splendors Portrayed, 76
But Solomon is not Happy, 77
Solomon's Riches, Wisdom and Wretchedness, 79
The City of David—Sorrow For Absalom, 80
The City of Great Temples, 82
Christ's Triumphant Entry, 83
Hosanna! Hosanna Cry the People, 85
The Scene From Olivet, 86
The City of Christ's Agony and Death. 88
The Last Sad Hour, 89
The New Jerusalem. 90

"THE STORMY PASSAGE ON GALILEE," 93
On the Banks of Galilee, 93
A Beautiful Scene, 94
On the Sea With Christ, 95
Christ Stilling the Tempest, 96
Have Christ on Your Ship, 96
The Martyrs, 99
Do Not be Frightened, 100
A Good Story of John Livingston, 103
Jesus is both God and Man, 104
Christ Can Hush the Tempest, 106

"A MARRIAGE FEAST." 109
The Wedding in Cana, 109

CONTENTS.

The Miracle at the Wedding,	110
The Wonderful Sympathy of Christ,	111
The Abundance of Christ's Giving,	112
Try to Make others Happy,	114
Christ Favors the Luxuries of Life,	115
Christ Does Not Deny us Joys,	116
Christ With us in Our Extremity—A Story,	119
Jesus Invites us to a Grander Wedding,	120
"THE SKY ANTHEM."	123
Christmas Eve in Palestine,	123
Indigency Not Degredation,	125
Duty and Blessing,	126
Religion is Joyful,	127
The Manger and Throne,	128
The Double Mission of Christ,	130
The Vision of Battles,	131
A Touching Story,	134
"THE HALF NOT TOLD.,,	137
The Two Circles,	137
A Vision of Beauty,	139
The Queen of Sheba,	140
Women, Wealth and Religion,	141
Earnestness in Search of Truth,	142
Religion a Surprise,	144
The Final Wonder,	146
"DOWNFALL OF ATHALIAH."	149
A Word to Grandmothers,	149
A Wife Steals a Child,	150
Righteousness Cannot be Exterminated,	152
Persecutions are Futile,	154
Infidelity Fails to Annihilate,	154
The Opportunities For Saving,	156
Persons in Your Sunday School Class,	158
How Phocus Dug His Grave and Died,	159
The Church is a Good Hiding Place,	160
Save Your Children,	163
"SALVATION BY FAITH."	167
The Crash of Earthquakes,	169
The Savior's Name,	170
The Wondrous Death,	172

CONTENTS.

A Story of a Young Man,	173
How to Trust Christ,	173
Saving Faith.	174
A Happy Life,	176
A Peaceful Death.	176
A Blissful Eternity,	178
A Mother's Story,	179
"THE NAME OF JESUS."	181
An Easy Name,	182
A Beautiful Name.	183
A Mighty Name,	186
An Enduring Name,	188
What Name Will You Call Christ?	189
O Come this Day to Christ.	192
"THE HOUSE ON THE WALL."	195
A Sad House,	196
Two Spies,	196
The Scarlet Thread,	198
Stretch this Scarlet Cord,	200
The First Step,	201
Protect Your Household,	203
My Good Mother,	204
The Scarlet Line at the Window.	205

ILLUSTRATIONS.

Rev. T. De Witt Talmage D. D.,	Frontispiece
Talmage's New Church Building,	1
The Old World,	16
Jerusalem and Solomon's Temple,	17
Trampling the Billows,	21
Tarsus the Birth Place of Paul,	30
The Storm,	34
Paul and Barnabas at Antioch;	37
The Golden Honr.	44
En Route,	46
The Ascension,	53
Unforgotten,	60
The Flood,	65
Mary and Martha,	69
A Cathedral Interior,	74
Ancient Jerusalem,	75
Jerusalem,	81
The Royal Rride to Jerusalem,	84
The Mount of Olives,	87
Jesus Crossing Galilee and Stilling the Tempest,	92
Saved in the Ark,	97
The Peaceful Little Home,	101
Jesus Healing the Blind,	105
Tropical Climes,	108
Christ Turning the Water into Wine,	109
"Enough For Every Brow a Chaplet,"	113
Sitting Under the Vine,	118
Song of the Angels,	122
The Star of Bethlehem,	123
The Babe in the Manger,	129
War in Ancient Times,	132
Bethlehem,	136
Earnest Seekers,	143
Napoleon Witnessing the Burning of Moscow,	148
Arc de Triumph, Paris,	149
Paul Before the Council,	153
Love of Children,	157
Jesus and the Doctors in the Temple,	161
Fleeing For the City of Refuge,	165
Abraham Offering His Son Isaac,	166
The Transfiguration,	167
Of Such is the Kingdom,"	180
The Peaceful River,	185
Symbol of the New Dispensation,	191
Rahab Concealing the Spies,	194
The Plains of Jericho,	199
The River of the Water of Life,	207

THE OLD WORLD.

PALESTINE SERMONS
— OF —
T. DE WITT TALMAGE, D. D.
Delivered during his tour of
THE ∴ HOLY ∴ LAND.

(JERUSALEM.)

LIFE'S GREAT VOYAGE.

[Delivered on board steamer "City of Paris," in New York harbor, October 29, 1889.]

"And they accompanied Him unto the ship." Acts xx, 38.

OFF FOR THE HOLY LAND.

TO the more than 25,000,000 people in many countries to whom my sermons come week by week in English tongue and by translation, through the kindness of the newspaper press, I address these words. I dictate them to a stenographer on the eve of my departure for the Holy land, Palestine. When you read this sermon I will be mid-atlantic.

I go to be gone a few weeks on a religious journey. I go because I want for myself and hearers and readers to see Bethlehem, and Nazareth, and Jerusalem, and Calvary, and all the other places connected with the Savior's life and death, and so reinforce myself for sermons. I go also because I am writing the "Life of Christ," and can be more accurate and graphic when I have been an eye-witness of the sacred places. Pray for my successful journey and my safe return.

I wish on the eve of my departure to pronounce a loving benediction upon all my friends in high places and low, upon congregations to whom my sermons are read in absence of pastors, upon groups gathered out on prairies and in mining districts, upon all sick and invalid and aged ones who cannot attend churches, but to whom I have long administered through the printed page. My next sermon will be addressed to you from Rome. I think I feel like Paul when he said: "So, as much as in me is, I am ready to preach the gospel to you that are at Rome also."

PAUL AS A SAILOR.

The fact is that Paul was ever moving about on land or sea. He was an old sailor—not from occupation, but from frequency of travel. I think he could have taken a vessel across the Mediterranean as well as some of the ship captains. The sailors never scoffed at him for being a "land lubber." If Paul's advice had been taken the crew would never have gone ashore at Melita.

When the vessel went scudding under bare poles Paul was the only self-possessed man on board, and, turning to the excited passengers, he exclaims in a voice that sounds above the thunder of the tempest and the wrath of the sea: "Be of good cheer."

ANCIENT NAVIGATION.

The men who now go to sea with maps, and charts, and modern compass, warned by buoys and light-house, know nothing of the perils of ancient navigation. Horace said that the man who first ventured on the sea must have had a heart bound with oak and triple brass. People then ventured only from headland to headland and from island to island, and not until long after spread their sail for a voyage across the sea. Before starting the weather was watched, and the vessel having been hauled up on the shore the mariners placed their shoulders against the stern of the ship and heaved it off, they at the last moment leaping into it. Vessels were then chiefly ships of burden—the transit of passengers being the exception; for the world was not then migratory as in our day, when the first desire of a man in one place seems to be to go into another place. The ship from which Jonah was thrown overboard and in that which Paul was carried prisoner went out chiefly with the idea of taking a cargo. As now, so then, vessels were accustomed to carry a flag. In those times it was inscribed with the name of a heathen deity. A vessel bound for Syracuse had on it the inscription "Castor and Pollux."

The ships were provided with anchors. Anchors were of two different kinds—those that were dropped into the sea and those that were thrown up onto the rocks to hold the vessel fast. This last kind was what Paul alluded to when he said: "Which hope we have as an anchor of the soul, both sure and steadfast, and which entereth into that within the vail." That was what the sailors call a "hook anchor." The rocks and sand-bars, shoals and headlands, not being mapped out, vessels carried a plumb line. They would drop it and find the water fifty fathoms, and drop it again and find it forty fathoms, and drop it again and find it thirty fathoms, thus discovering their near approach to the shore.

TRAMPLING THE BILLOWS.

In the spring, summer, and autumn, the Mediterranean sea was white with the wings of ships, but at the first wintry blast they hied themselves to the nearest harbor, although now the world's commerce prospers in January as well as in June, and in mid-winter all over the wide and stormy deep there floats palaces of light, trampling the billows under foot and showering the sparks of terrible furnaces on the wild wind, and the Christian passenger, tippeted and shawled, sits under the shelter of the smoke-stack, looking off upon the phosphorescent deep, on which is written in scrolls of foam and fire: "Thy way, O God, is in the sea and thy path in the great waters!"

It is in those days of early navigation that I see a group of men, women, and children on the beach of the Mediterranean. Paul is about to leave the congregation to whom he had preached and they are come down to see him off. It is a solemn thing to part. There are so many traps that wait for a man's feet. The solid ground may break through, and the sea—how many dark mysteries it hides in its bosom! A few counsels, a hasty good-by, a last look, and the ropes rattle, and the sails are hoisted, and the planks are

hauled in, and Paul is gone. I expect to sail over some of the same waters over which Paul sailed, but before going I want to urge you all to embark for heaven.

THE CHURCH IS THE DRY DOCK FOR REPAIRS.

The church is the dry dock where souls are to be fitted out for heaven. In making a vessel for this voyage the first need is sound timber. The floor timbers ought to be of solid stuff. For the want of it vessels that look able to run their jibbooms into the eye of any tempest when caught in a storm have been crushed like a wafer. The truths of God's word are what I mean by floor timbers. Away with your lighter materials. Nothing but oaks hewn in the forest of divine truth, are staunch enough for this craft.

LOVE IS THE HELM.

You must have love for a helm to guide and turn the craft. Neither pride nor ambition nor avarice will do for a rudder. Love, not only in the heart, but flashing in the eye and tingling in the hand—love married to work, which many look upon as so homely a bride—love, not like brooks, which foam and rattle, yet do nothing, but love like a river, that runs up the steps of mill-wheels and works in the harness of factory bands—love that will not pass by on the other side, but visits the man who fell among thieves near Jericho, not merely saying; "Poor fellow! you are dreadfully hurt," but like the good Samaritan, pours in oil and wine and pays his board at the tavern. There must also be a prow, aranged to cut and override the billow. That is Christian perservance. There are three mountain surges that sometimes dash againist a soul in a minute—the world, the flesh and the devil—and that is a well built prow that can bound over them. For lack of this many have put back and never started again. It is the broadside wave that so often sweeps the deck and fills the hatches, but that which strikes in front is harmless. Meet troubles courageously and you surmount them. Stand on the prow, and as you wipe off the spray of the split surge, cry out with the apostle: "None of these things move me." Let all your fears stay aft. The right must conquer. Know that Moses, in an ark of bulrushes, can run down a war-steamer.

THE ANCHOR IS HOPE.

Have a good, strong anchor. "Which hope we have as an anchor." By this strong cable and windlass hold on to your anchor. "If any man sin we have an advocate with the father." Do not use the anchor wrongfully. Do not always stay in the same latitude and longitude. You will never ride up the harbor of eternal rest if you all the way drag your anchor.

FAITH IS OUR CANVAS.

But you must have sails. Vessels are not fit for the sea until they have the flying jib, the foresail, the top gallant, the skysail, the gaffsail, and other canvas. Faith is our canvas. Hoist it and the winds of heaven will drive you ahead. Sails made out of any other canvas than faith will be split to tatters by the first northeaster. Strong faith never lost a battle. It will crush foes, blast rocks, quench lightnings, thrash mountains. It is a shield to the warrior, a crank to the most ponderous wheel, a lever to pry up pyramids, a drum whose beat gives strength to the heavenly soldiery, and sails to waft ships laden with priceless pearls from the harbor of earth to the harbor of heaven.

PRAYER THE RUNNING RIGGING.

But you are not yet equipped. You must have what seamen call the running rigging. This comprises the ship's braces, halyards, clew-lines, and such like. Without these the yards could not be braced, the sails lifted, or the canvas in anywise managed. We have prayer for the running rigging. Unless you understand this tackling you are not a spiritual seaman. By pulling on these ropes you hoist the sails of faith and turn them every whither. The prow of courage will not cut the wave nor the sail of faith spread and flap its wings unless you have a strong prayer for a halyard.

THE COMPASS IS THE BIBLE.

One more arrangement and you will be ready for sea. You must have a compass—which is a bible. Look at it every day, and always sail by it, as its needle points toward the star of Bethehem. Through fog, and darkness, and storm it works faithfully. Search the scriptures. "Box the compass."

Let me give you two or three rules for the voyage. Allow your appetites and passions only an under-deck passage. Do not allow them ever to come up on the promenade deck. Mortify your members which are upon the earth. Never allow your lower nature anything better than a steerage passage. Let watchfulness walk the decks as an armed sentinel and shoot down with great promptness anything like a munity of riotous appetites.

LOOKOUT FOR ICE-BERGS.

Be sure to look out of the forecastle for icebergs. There are cold christians floating around in the church. The frigid-zone professors will sink you. Stear clear of icebergs. Keep a log-book during all the voyage—an account of how many furlongs you make a day. The merchant keeps a day-book as well as a ledger. You ought to know every night, as well as every year, how things are going. When the express train stops at the depot you hear a hammer sounding on the wheels, thus testing the safety of the rail train. Bound as we are with more than express speed toward a great eternity, ought we not often to try the work of self-examination?

KEEP YOUR COLORS UP.

Be sure to keep your colors up. You know the ships of England, Russia, France and Spain by the ensigns they carry. Sometimes it is a lion, sometimes an eagle, sometimes a star, sometimes a crown. Let it ever be known who you are and for what port you are bound. Let "Christian" be written on the very front, with a figure of a cross, a crown, and a dove, and from the masthead let float the streamers of Immanuel. Then the pirate vessels of temptation will pass you by unharmed as they say: "There goes a Christian, bound for the port of heaven. We will not disturb her, for she has too many guns aboard."

Run up your flag on this pully: "I am not ashamed of the gospel of Christ, for it is the power of God and the wisdom of God unto salvation." When driven back or laboring under great stress of weather—now changing from starboard tack to larboard, and then from larboard to starboard—look above the topgallants and your heart shall beat like a war-drum as the streamers float on the wind. The sign of the cross will make you patient and the crown will make you glad.

CHRIST IS THE PILOT.

Before you gain port you will smell the land breezes of heaven, and Christ the pilot, will meet you as you come into the narrows of death, and fasten to you, and say: "When thou passest through the waters I will be with thee; and through the rivers, they shall not overflow thee." Are you ready for such a voyage? Make up your minds. The gang-planks are lifting. The bell rings. All aboard for heaven! This world is not your rest. The chaffinch is the silliest bird in all the earth for trying to make its nest on the rocking billow. Oh, how I wish that as I embark for the Holy land in the east, all to whom I preach by tongue or type would embark for heaven! What you all most need is God, and you need him now. Some of you I leave in trouble. Things are going very rough with you. You have had a hard struggle with poverty, or sickness, or persecution, or bereavement. Light after light has gone out, and it is so dark that you can hardly see any blessing left. May that Jesus who comforted the widow of Nain and raised the deceased to life, with his gentle hand of sympathy wipe away your tears! All is well.

INCIDENTS IN THE LIFE OF DAVID, JOB, ROSSINI AND WATTS.

When David was fleeing through the wilderness pursued by his own son he was being prepared to become the sweet singer of Israel. The pit and the dungeon were the best schools at which Joseph ever graduated. The hurricane that upset the tent and killed Job's children prepared the man of Uz to write the magnificent poem that has astonished the ages. There is no way to get the wheat out of the straw but to thrash it. There is no way to purify the gold but to burn it. Look at the people who have always had it their own way. They are proud, discontented, useless, and unhappy. If you want to find cheerful folks go among those who have been purified by the fire. After Rossini had rendered "William Tell" the five hundreth time a company of musicians came under his window in Paris and serenaded him. They put upon his brow a golden crown of laurel leaves. But amidst all the applause and enthusiasm Rossini turned to a friend and said: "I would give all this brilliant scene for a few days of youth and love." Contrast the melancholy feeling of Rossini, who had everything that this world could give him, to the joyful experience of Isaac Watts, whose misfortunes were innumerable, when he says:

> "The hill of Zion yields
>   A thousand sacred sweets
> Before we reach the heavenly fields,
>   Or walk the golden streets.
>
> Then let our songs abound,
>   And every tear be dry;
> We're marching through Immanuel's ground,
>   To fairer worlds on high."

It is prosperity that kills and trouble that saves. While the Israelites were on the march, amid great privations and hardships, they behaved well. After a while they prayed for meat, and the sky darkened with a large flock of quails, and these quails fell in great multitudes all about them; and the Israelites ate and ate and they stuffed themselves until they died. Oh!

my friends, it is not hardship, or trial, or starvation that injures the soul, but abundant supply. It is not the vulture of trouble that eats up the Christian's life; it is the quails! it is the quails!

ONCE MORE I CONFESS MY FAITH.

I can not leave you until once more I confess my faith in the Savior whom I have preached. He is my all in all. I owe more to the grace of God than most men. With this ardent temperament if I had gone over-board I would have gone to the very depths. You know I can do nothing by halves:

> "Oh, to grace how great a debtor
> Daily I'm constrained to be!"

I think all will be well. Do not be worried about me. I know that my Redeemer liveth, and if any fatality should befall me I think I should go straight. I have been most unworthy, and would be sorry to think that any one of my friends had been as unworthy a Christian as myself. But God has helped a great many through, and I hope he will help me through. It is a long account of shortcomings, but if he is going to rub any of it out I think he will rub it all out. And now give us (for I go not alone) your benediction. When you send letters to a friend in a distant land you say via such a city or via such a steamer. When you send your good wishes to us send them via the throne of God. We shall not travel out of the reach of your prayers:

> "There is a scene where spirits blend,
> Where friend holds intercourse with friend;
> Though sundered far, by faith we meet
> Around one common mercy seat."

"GOOD-BY."

And now, may the blessing of God come down upon your bodies and upon your souls, your fathers and mothers, your companions, your children your brothers and sisters, and your friends! May you be blessed in your business and in your pleasures, in your joys and in your sorrows, in the house and by the way! And if, during our separation, an arrow from the unseen world should strike any of us, may it only hasten on the raptures that God has prepared for those who love him! I utter not the word farewell; it is too sad, too formal a word for me to speak or write. But, considering that I have your hand tightly clasped in mine, I utter a kind, an affectionate, and a cheerful good-by!

TARSUS, THE BIRTHPLACE OF PAUL. (30)

IN BRINDISI.

A MEDITERRANEAN VOYAGE.

[Delivered in Brindisi, an Italian port, Nov. 17, 1889.]

"And so it came to pass that they escaped all safe to land."
Acts xxvii, 44.

THE APPIAN WAY—PAUL AS A "SIGNAL OFFICER."

AVING visited your historical city, which we desired to see because it was the terminus of the most famous road of the ages, the Roman Appian Way, and for its mighty fortress overshadowing a city which even Hannibal's hosts could not thunder down, we must to-morrow morning leave your harbor, and, after touching at Athens and Corinth, voyage about the Mediterranean to Alexandria, Egypt.

I have been reading this morning in my New Testament of a Mediterranean voyage in an Alexandrian ship. It was this very month of November. The vessel was lying in a port not very far from here. On board that vessel were two distinguished passengers: one, Josephus, the historian, as we have strong reasons to believe; the other, a convict, one Paul by name, who was going to prison for upsetting things, or, as they termed it, "turning the world upside down." This convict had gained the confidence of the captain. Indeed, I think that Paul knew almost as much about the sea as did the captain. He had been shipwrecked three times already; he had dwelt much of his life amidst capstans, and yardarms, and cables, and storms, and he knew what he was talking about. Seeing the equinoctial storm was coming, and perhaps noticing something unseaworthy in the vessel, he advised the captain to stay in the harbor. But I heard the captain and the first mate talking together. They say: "We cannot afford to take the advice of this landsman and he a minister. He may be able to preach very well, but I don't believe he knows a marlinespike from a luff tackle. All aboard! Cast off! Shift the helm for headway! Who fears the Mediterranean? They had gone only a little way out when a whirlwind, called Euroclydon, made the torn sail its turban, shook the mast as you would brandish a spear, and tossed the hulk into the heavens. Overboard with the cargo! It is all washed with salt water and worthless now, and there are no marine insurance companies. All hands, ahoy, and out with the anchors!

AN EXCITED CREW.

Great consternation comes on crew and passengers. The sea monsters snort in the foam, and the billows clap their hands in glee of destruction. In the lull of the storm I hear a chain clank. It is the chain of the great apostle as he walks the deck, or holds fast to the rigging amidst the lurching of the ship—the spray dripping from his long beard as he cries out to the crew: "Now I exhort you to be of good cheer, for there shall be no loss of any man's life among you, but of the ship. For there stood by me this night the angel of God, whose I am, and whom I serve, saying, fear not, Paul, thou must be brought before Cæsar; and lo, God hath given thee all them that sail with thee."

Fourteen days have passed and there is no abatement of the storm. It is midnight. Standing on the lookout, the man peers into the darkness, and, by a flash of lightning, sees the long white line of breakers, and knows they must be coming near to some country, and fears that in a few moments the vessel will be shivered on the rocks.

AN AWFUL SHIPWRECK.

The ship flies like chaff in the tornado. They drop the the sounding line, and by the light of the lantern they see it is twenty fathoms. Speeding along a little farther, they drop the line again, and by the light of the lantern they see it is fifteen fathoms. Two hundred and seventy-six souls within a few feet of awful shipwreck! The managers of the vessel, pretending they want to look over the side of the ship and undergird it, get into the small boat, expecting in it to escape; but Paul sees through the sham, and he tells them that if they go off

in the boat it will be the death of them. The vessel strikes! The planks spring! The timbers crack! The vessel parts in the thundering surge! Oh. what wild struggling for life! Here they leap from plank, to plank. Here they go under as if they would never rise, but, catching hold of a timber, come floating and panting on it to the beach. Here, strong swimmers spread their arms through the waves until their chins plow the sand, and they rise up and wring out their wet locks on the beach. When the roll of the ship is called two hundred and seventy-six people answer to their names. "And so,', says my text, "it came to pass that they escaped all safe to land." I learn from this subject.

TEMPTERS ARE NOT HELPERS.

First, that those who get us into trouble will not stay to help us out. These shipmen got Paul out of Fair Havens into the storm.; but as soon as the tempest dropped upon them they wanted to go off in the small boat, caring nothing what became of Paul and the passengers. Ah me! human nature is the same in all ages. They who get us into trouble never stop to help us out. They who tempt that young man into a life of dissipation will be the first to laugh at his imbecility, and to drop him out of decent society. Gamblers always make fun of the losses of gamblers. They who tempt you in to the contest with fists, saying, "I will back you," will be the first to run. Look over all the predicaments of your life, and count the names of those who have got you into those predicaments, and tell me the name of one who ever helped you out. They were glad enough to get you out from Fair Havens, but when, with damaged rigging, you try to get into harbor, did they hold for you a plank or throw you a rope? Not one. Satan has got thousands of men into trouble, but he would not hide the goods or bail out the defendant. The spider shows the fly the way over the gossamer bridge in to the cobweb; but it never shows the fly the way out of the cobweb over the gossamer bridge. I think that there were plenty of fast young men to help the prodigal spend his money; but when he had wasted his substance in riotous living, they let him go to the swine pastures, while they betook themselves to some other new comer. They who take Paul out of Fair Havens will be of no help to him when he gets into the breakers of Melita.

DANGEROUS TO REFUSE GOOD ADVICE.

I remark again, as a lesson learned from the text, that it is dangerous to refuse the counsel of competent advisers. Paul told them not to go out with that ship. They thought he knew nothing about it. They said: "He is only a minister!" They went, and the ship was destroyed. There are a great many people who now say of ministers: "They know nothing about the world. They cannot talk to us!" Ah, my friends, it is not necessary to have the Asiatic cholera before you can give it medical treatment in others. It is not necessary to have your own arm broken before you can know how to splinter a fracture. And we who stand in the pulpit, and in the office of a Christian teacher, know that there are certain styles of belief and certain kinds of behavior that will lead to destructiou as certainly as Paul knew that if that ship went out Fair Havens it would go to destruction. "Rejoice, O young man, in thy youth; and let thy heart cheer thee in the days of thy youth; but know thou that for all these things God will bring

PAUL AND BARNABAS AT ANTIOCH.

thee into judgment." We may not know much, but we know that.

Young people refuse the advice of parents. They say: "Father is over-suspicious, and mother is getting old." But those parties have been on the sea of life. They know where the storms sleep, and during their voyage have seen a thousand battered hulks marking the place where beauty burned. and intellect foundered, and morality sank. They are old sailors, having answered many a signal of distress and endured great stress of weather, and gone scudding under bare poles; and the old folks know what they are talking about. Look at that man—in his cheek the glow of internal fires. His eyes flash not as once with thought, but with low passion. His brain is a sewer through which impurity floats, and his heart the trough in which lusts wallows and drinks. Men shudder as the leper passes, and parents cry, "Wolf! wolf!" Yet he once said the Lord's Prayer at his mother's knee, and against that iniquitous brow once pressed a pure mother's lip. But he refused her counsel. He went where euroclydons have their lair. He foundered on the sea, while all hell echoed at the roar of the wreck: Lost Pacifics! Lost Pacifics! You have, my friends, had illustrations, in your own life, of how God delivers his people. I have had illustrations in my own life of the same truth.

IN A CYCLONE ON THE SEA.

I was once in what on your Mediterranean you call a Euroclydon; but what on the Atlantic we call a cyclone, but the same storm. The steamer Greece of the National Line, swung out into the River Mersey at Liverpool, bound for New York. We had on board seven hundred, crew and passengers. We came together strangers—

Italians, Irishmen, Englishmen, Swedes, Norwegians, Americans. Two flags floated from the masts—British and American ensigns. We had a new vessel, or one so thoroughly remodeled that the voyage had around it all the uncertainties of a trial trip. The steamer felt its way cautiously out into the sea. The pilot was discharged, and, committing ourselves to the care of him who holdeth the winds in his fists, we were fairly started on our voyage of three thousand miles. It was rough nearly all the way—the sea with strong buffeting disputing our path. But one night at 11 o'clock, after the lights had been put out, a cyclone—a wind just made to tear ships to pieces—caught us up in its clutches. It came down so suddenly that we had not time to take in the sails or to fasten the hatches. You may know that the bottom of the Atlantic is strewn with the ghastly work of cyclones. Oh! they are cruel winds.

I thought that I had seen storms on the sea before; but all of them together might have come under one wing of that cyclone. We were only eight or nine hundred miles from home, and in high expectation of soon seeing our friends, for there was no one on board so poor as not to have a friend. But it seemed as if we were to be disappointed.

WE EXPECTED TO DIE.

The most of us expected then and there to die. There were none who made light of the peril, save two. One was an Englishman, and he was drunk, and the other was an American, and he was a fool! Oh! wat a time it was! A night to make one's hair to turn white. We came out of the berths and stood in the gangway, and looked into the steerage, and sat in the cabin. While seated there we heard overhead something like minute guns. It was the bursting of the sails. We held on with both hands to keep our places. Those who attempted to cross the floor came back bruised and gashed. Cups and glasses were dashed to fragments: pieces of the table getting loose, swung across the saloon. It seemed as if the hurricane took that great ship of thousands of tons and stood it on end and said: "Shall I sink it, or let go this once?" And then it came down with such force that the billows trampled over it, each mounted of a fury. We felt that everything depended on the propelling screw. If that stopped for an instant we knew the vessel would fall off into the trough of the sea and sink, and so we prayed that the screw, which three times since leaving Liverpool had already stopped, might not stop now. Oh! how anxiously we listened for the regular thump of the machinery, upon which our lives seemed to depend. After awhile some one said: "The screw is stopped!" No, its sound had only been overpowered by the uproar of the tempest, and we breathed easier again when we heard the regular pulsation of the overtasked machinery going thump, thump, thump.

THE TERRIFIED PASSENGERS.

There were about five hundred and fifty passengers in the steerage, and as the water rushed in and touched the furnaces, and began violently to hiss, the poor creatures in the steerage imagined that the boilers were giving way. Those passengers writhed in the water and in the mud some praying, some crying, all terrified. They made a rush for the deck. An officer stood on deck and beat them back with blow after blow. It was necessary. They could not have stood an instant on the deck. Oh! how they begged to get out of the hold of the ship! One woman, with a child in her arms, rushed up and caught hold of one the officers and cried: "Do let me out! I cannot die here!" Some got down and prayed to the Virgin Mary, saying: "Oh blessed mother! keep us! Have mercy on us!" Some stood with white lips and fixed gaze, silent in their terror. Some wrung their hands and cried out: "Oh God! What shall I do? What shall I do?" The time came when the crew could no longer stay on the deck, and the cry of the officers was: "Below! all hands below!" Our brave and sympathetic Captain Andrews—whose praise I shall not cease to speak while I live—had been swept by the hurricane from his bridge, and had escaped very narrowly with his life.

WILD CRY OF THE CYCLONE.

The cyclone seemed to stand on the deck, waving its wing, crying: "This ship is mine! I have captured it! Ha! Ha! I will command it! If God will permit I will sink it here and now. By a thousand shipwrecks, I swear the doom of this vessel!" There was a lull in the storm, but only that it might gain additional fury. Crash! went the lifeboat on one side. Crash! went the lifeboat on the other side. The great booms got loose, and, as with the heft of the thunderbolt, pounded the deck and beat the mast—the jibboom, studdingsail boom, and square sail boom, with their strong arms, beating time to the awful march and music of the hurricane.

Meanwhile the ocean became phosphorescent. The whole scene looked like fire. The water dripping from the rigging, there were ropes of fire; and there were masts of fire; and there was a deck of fire. A ship of fire, sailing on a sea of fire, through a night of fire. May I never see anything like it again! Everybody prayed. A lad of twelve years of age got down and prayed for his mother. "If I should give up," he said, "I do not know what would become of mother." There were men also, I think had not prayed for thirty years, who then got down on their knees. When a man who has neglected God all his life feels that, he has come to his last time, it makes a very busy night. All of our sins and shortcomings passed through our minds.

MY DYING PRAYER.

My own life seemed utterly unsatisfactory. I could only say, "Here, Lord, take me as I am. I cannot mend matters now. Lord Jesus, thou didst die for the chief of sinners. That's me! It seems, Lord, as if my work is done, and poorly done, and upon thy infinite mercy I cast myself, and in this hour of shipwreck and darkness commit myself and her whom I hold by the hand to thee, O Lord Jesus! praying that it may be a short struggle in the water, and that at the same instant we may both arrive in glory!" Oh! I tell you a man prays straight to the mark when he has a cyclone above him, an ocean beneath him, and eternity so close to him that he can feel its breath on his cheek.

The night was long. At last we saw the dawn, looking through the portholes. As in the olden time, in the fourth watch of the night, Jesus came walking on the sea, from wave cliff to wave cliff; and when he puts his foot upon a billow, though it may be tossed up with might, it goes down. He cried to the winds, Hush! They knew his voice. The waves knew his foot. They died away. And in the shining track of his feet I read these letters on scrolls of foam and fire, "The earth shall be filled with the knowledge of God as the waters cover the sea."

THE BEAUTIFUL MORNING.

The ocean calmed. The path of the steamer became more and more mild; until, on the last morning out, the sun threw around about us a glory such as I never witnessed before. God made a pavement of mosaic, reaching from horizon to horizon, for all the splendors of earth and heaven to walk upon—a pavement bright enough for the foot of a seraph—bright enough for the wheels of the archangel's chariot. As a parent embraces a child, and kisses away its grief, so over that sea that had been writhing in agony in the tempest, the morning threw its arms of beauty and of benediction, and the lips of earth and heaven met.

As I came on deck—it was very early, and we were nearing the shore—I saw a few sails against the sky. They seemed like the spirits of the night walking the billows. I leaned over the taffrail of the vessel, and said, "Thy way, O God, is in the sea, and thy path in the great waters."

It grew lighter. The clouds were hung in purple clusters along the sky; and, as if those purple clusters were pressed into red wine and poured out upon the sea, every wave turned into crimson. Yonder, fire cleft stood opposite to fire cleft; and here, a cloud, rent and tinged with light, seemed like a palace, with flames bursting from the windows. The whole scene lighted up until it seemed as if the angels of God were ascending and descending upon stairs of fire, and the wavecrests, changed into jasper, and crystal, and amethyst, as they

were flung toward the beach, made me think of the crowns of heaven cast before the throne of the great Jehovah. I leaned over the taffrail again and said, with more emotion than before: "Thy way, O God, is in the sea, and thy path in the great waters!",

THE GLORIFIED SHORE.

So, I thought, will be the going off of the storm and night of the Christian's night. The darkness will fold its tents and away! The golden feet of the rising morn will come skipping upon the mountains, and all the wrathful billows of the world's woe break into the splendor of eternal joy. And so we come into the harbor. The cyclone behind us. Our friends all before us. God, who is always good, all around us. And if the roll of the crew and the passengers had been called, seven hundred souls would have answered to their names. "And so it came to pass that we all escaped safe to land."

And may God grant that, when all our Sabbaths on earth are ended, we may find that, in the rich mercy of our Lord Jesus Christ, we all have weathered the gale!"

> Into the harbor of heaven now we glide,
> Home at last!
> Softly we drift on the bright silver tide,
> Home at last!
> Glory to God! All our dangers are o'er;
> We stand secure on the glorified shore.
> Glory to God! We will shout evermore,
> Home at last!
> Home at last!

EN ROUTE.

IN ATHENS.

THE CLOUDED VISION.

[Delivered in Athens, Greece, November 24, 1889.]

"*Eye hath not seen, nor ear heard.*" *I Cor.*, ii, 9.
"*For now we see through a glass darkly.*" *I Cor.*, xiii, 12.

THE ILLUSTRIOUS PAUL.

BOTH these sentences were written by the most illustrious merely human being the world ever saw, one who walked these streets, and preached from yonder pile of rocks, Mars Hill. Though more classic associations are connected with this city than with any city under the sun, because here Socrates, and Plato, and Aristotle, and Demosthenes, and Pericles, and Heroditus, and Pythagoras, and Xenophon, and Praxiteles wrote or chiseled, or taught or thundered or sung, yet in my mind all those men and their teachings were eclipsed by Paul and the Gospel he preached in this city and in your nearby city of Corinth. Yesterday, standing on the old fortress at Corinth, the Acro-Corinthus, out from the ruins at is base arose in my imagination the old city, just as Paul saw it.

THE SPLENDOR OF ANCIENT CORINTH.

I have been told that, for splendor the world beholds no such wonder today as that ancient Corinth standing on an isthmus washed by two seas, the one sea bringing the commerce of Europe, the other sea bringing the commerce of Asia. From her wharves, in the construction of which whole kingdoms had been absorbed, war galleys with three banks of oars pushed out and confounded the navy yards of all the world. Huge handed machinery, such as modern invention cannot equal, lifted ships from the sea on one side and transported them on trucks across the isthmus and sat them down in the sea on the other side. The revenue officers of the city went down through the olive groves that lined the beach to collect a tariff from all nations. The mirth of all people sported in her Isthmain games, and the beauty of all lands sat in her theatres, walked her porticos and threw itself on the altar of her stupendous dissipations. Column, and statue, and temple bewildered the beholder. There were white marble fountains, into which, from apertures at the side, there gushed waters everywhere known for health giving qualities. Around these basins, twisted into wreaths of stone, there were all the beauties of sculpture and architecture; while standing, as if to guard the costly display, was a statue of Hercules of burnished Corinthian brass. Vases of terra cotta adorned the cemeteries of the dead—vases so costly that Julius Cæsar was not satisfied until he had captured them for Rome. Armed officials, the corinthian, paced up and down to see that no statue was defaced, or pedestal overthrown, no bas-relief touched. From the edge of the city the hill held its magnificent burden of columns and towers and temples (1,000 slaves waiting at one shrine), and a citadel so thoroughly impregnable that Gibraltar is a heap of sand compared with it. Amid all that strength and magnificence Corinth stood and defied the world.

PAUL ADDRESSED THE HIGHEST CULTURE.

Oh! it was not to rustics who had never seen anything grand that Paul uttered one of my texts. They had heard the best music that had come from the best instruments in all the world; they had heard songs floating from morning porticos and melting in evening groves; they had past their whole lives among pictures and sculpture and architecture and Corinthian brass, which had been molded and shaped until there was no chariot wheel in which it had not sped, and no tower in which it had not glittered, and no gateway that it had not adorned. Ah, it was a bold thing for Paul to stand there amid all that and say: "All this is nothing. These sounds that come from the temple of Neptune are not music compared with the harmonies of which I speak. These waters rushing in the basin of Pyrene are not pure. These statues of Bacchus and Mercury are not exquisite. Your citadel of Acro-Corinthus is not strong compared with that which I offer to the poorest slave that puts down his burden at that brazen gate.

You Corinthians think this is a splendid city; you think you have heard all sweet sounds and seen all beautiful sights; but I tell you eye hath not seen nor ear heard, neither have entered into the heart of man, the things which God hath prepared for them that love him. Indeed both my texts, the one spoken by Paul and the one written by Paul, show us that we have very imperfect eyesight, and that our day of vision is yet to come: for now we see through a glass, darkly, but then face to face. So Paul takes the responsibility of saying that even the Bible is an indistinct mirror, and that its mission shall be finally suspended.

I think there may be one Bible in heaven fastened to the throne. Just as now, in a museum, we have a lamp exhumed from Herculaneum or Nineveh, and we look at it with great interest and say: "How poor a light it must have given, compared with our modern lamps," so I think that this Bible, which was a lamp to our feet in this world, may lie near the throne of God, exciting our interest to all eternity by the contrast between its comparatively feeble light and the illumination of heaven. The Bible, now, is the scaffolding to the rising temple, but when the building is done there will be no use for the scaffolding.

OUR DIM VISION WILL GROW BRIGHTER.

The idea I shall develope today is, that in this world our knowledge is comparatively dim and unsatisfactory, but nevertheless is introductory to grander and more complete vision.

THIS IS TRUE OF OUR KNOWLEDGE OF GOD.

This is eminently true in regard to our view of God. We hear so much about God that we conclude that we understand him. He is represented as having the tenderness of a father, the firmness of a judge, the pomp of a king and the love of a mother. We hear about him, talk about him, write about him. We lisp his name in infancy, and it trembles on the tongue of the dying octogenarian. We think that we know very much about him. Take the attribute of mercy. Do we understand it? The Bible blossoms all over with that word, mercy. It speaks again and again of the tender mercies of God, of the sure mercies, of the great mercies, of the mercies that endureth for ever, of the multitude of his mercies. And yet I know that the views we have of this great being are most indefinite, one sided and incomplete. When, at death. the gates shall fly open, and we shall look directly npon him, how new and surprising.

We see upon canvas a picture of the morning. We study the cloud in the sky, the dew upon the grass, and the husbandman on the way to the field. Beautiful picture of the morning! But we arise at daybreak, and go up on a hill to see for ourselves that which was represented to us. While we look, the mountains are transfigured. The burnished gates of heaven swing open and shut, to let pass a host of fiery splendors. The clouds are abloom, and hang pendant from arbors of alabaster and amethyst. The waters make pathway of inlaid pearl for the light to walk upon; and there is morning on the sea. The crags uncover their scarred visage; and there is morning among the mountains. Now you go home, and how tame your picture of the morning seems in contrast? Greater than that shall be the contrast between this scriptural view of God and that which we shall have when standing face to face. This is a picture of the morning; that will be the morning itself.

AND TRUE OF THE SAVIOUR'S EXCELLENCY.

Again: My texts are true of the Saviour's excellency. By image, and sweet rhythm of expression, and startling antitheses, Christ is set forth—his love, his compassion, his work, his life, his death, his resurrection. We are challenged to measure it, to compute it, to weigh it. In the hour of our broken enthrallment, we mount up into high experience of his love, and shout until the countenance glows, and the blood bounds, and the whole nature is exhilarated. "I have found him." And yet it is through a glass, darkly. We see not half of that compassionate face. We feel not half the warmth of that loving heart. We wait for death to let us rush into his outspread arms. Then we shall be face to face. Not shadow then, but substance. Not hope then, but the fulfilling of all prefigurement. That will be a magnificent unfolding.

The rushing out in view of all hidden excellency; the coming again of a long-absent Jesus to meet us—not in rags and in penury and death, but amidst a light and pomp and outbursting joy such as none but a glorified intelligence could experience. Oh! to gaze full upon the brow that was lacerated, upon the side that was pierced, upon the feet that were nailed; to stand close up in the presence of him who prayed for us on the mountain, and thought of us by sea, and agonized for us in the garden, and died for us in horrible crucifixion; to feel of him, to embrace him, to take his hand, to kiss his feet, to run our fingers along the scars of ancient suffering; to say: "This is my Jesus! He gave himself for me. I shall forever behold his glory. I shall eternally hear his voice. Lord Jesus, now I see thee. I behold where the blood started, where the tears coursed, where the face was distorted. I have waited for this hour. I shall never turn my back on thee. No more looking through imperfect glasses. No more studying thee in the darkness. But, as long as this throne stands, and this everlasting

THE ASCENSION.

river flows, and those garlands bloom, and these arches of victory remain to greet home heaven's conquerors, so long I shall see thee, Jesus of my choice; Jesus of my song; Jesus of my triumph—forever and forever—face to face!"

GOD'S PROVIDENCES NOT UNDERSTOOD FULLY NOW, BUT WILL BE HEREAFTER.

The idea of my texts is just as true when applied to God's providence. Who has not come to some pass in life thoroughly inexplicable? You say: "What does this mean? What is God going to do with me now? He tells me that all things work together for good. This does not look like it." You continue to study the dispensation, and after a while guess about what God means. "He means to teach me this. I think he means to teach me that. Perhaps it is to humble my pride. Perhaps it is to make me feel more dependent. Perhaps to teach me the uncertainty of life." But after all, it is only a guess—a looking through the glass, darkly. The Bible assures us there shall be a satisfactory unfolding. "What I do thou knowest not now; but thou shalt know hereafter." You will know why God took to himself that only child. Next door there was a household of seven children. Why not take one from that group, instead of your only one? Why single out the dwelling in which there was only one heart beating responsive to yours? Why did God give you a child at all, if he meant to take it away? Why fill the cup of your gladness brimming, if he meant to dash it down? Why allow all the tendrils of your heart to wind around that object, and then, when every fiber of your own life seemed to be interlocked with the child's life, with strong hand to tear you apart, until you fall bleeding and crushed, your dwelling desolate, your hopes blasted, your heart broken? Do you suppose that God will explain that? Yea. He will make it plainer than any mathematical problem—as plain as that two and two make four. In the light of the throne you will see that it was right—all right. "Just and true are all thy ways, thou King of saints."

PROVIDENTIAL HINDRANCES IN LIFE.

Here is a man who cannot get on in the world. He always seems to buy at the wrong time and to sell at the worst disadvantage. He tries this enterprise, and fails; that business, and is disappointed. The man next door to him has a lucrative trade, but he lacks customers. A new prospect opens. His income is increased. But that year his family are sick; and the profits are expended in trying to cure the ailments. He gets a discouraged look. Becomes faithless as to success. Begins to expect disasters. Others wait for something to turn up; he waits for it to turn down. Others, with only half as much education and character, get on twice as well. He sometimes guesses as to what it all means. He says: "Perhaps riches would spoil me. Perhaps poverty is necessary to keep me humble. Perhaps I might, if things were otherwise, be tempted into dissipations." But there is no complete solution of the mystery. He sees through a glass, darkly, and must wait for a higher unfolding. Will there be an explanation? Yes; God will take that man in the light of the throne, and say: "Child immortal, hear the explanation! You remember the failing of that great enterprise. This is the explanation." And you will answer: "It is all right!"

I see, every day, profound mysteries of Providence. There is no question we ask oftener than Why? There are hundreds of graves that need to be explained. Hospitals for the blind and lame, asylums for the idiotic and insane, almshouses for the destitute, and a world of pain and misfortune that demand more than human solution. Ah! God will clear it all up. In the light that pours from the throne, no dark mystery can live.

Things now utterly inscrutable will be illumined as plainly as if the answer were written on the jasper wall, or sounded in the temple anthem. Bartimeus will thank God that he was blind; and Lazarus that he was covered with sores; and Joseph that he was cast into the pit; and Daniel that he denned with lions; and Paul that he was humpbacked; and David that he was driven from Jerusalem; and the sewing-woman that she could only get a few pence for making a garment; and that invalid that for twenty years he could not lift his head from the pillow; and that widow that she had such hard work to earn bread for her children. You know that in a song different voices carry different parts. The sweet and overwhelming part of the hallelujah of heaven will not be carried by those who rode in high places. and gave sumptuous entertainments; but pauper children will sing it, beggars will sing it, redeemed hod-carriers will sing it, those who were once the offscouring of earth will sing it. The hallelujah will be all the grander for the earth's weeping eyes, and aching heads, and exhausted hands, and scourged back, and martyred agonies.

HOW MANY SHALL BE SAVED?

Again: The thought of my texts is true when applied to the enjoyment of the righteous in heaven. I think we have but little idea of the number of the righteous in heaven. Infidels say: "Your heaven will be a very small place compared with the world of the lost; for, according to your teaching, the majority of men will be destroyed." I deny the charge. I suppose that the multitude of the finally lost, as compared with the multitude of the finally saved, will be a hand full. I suppose that the few sick people in the hospitals of our great cities, as compared with the hundreds of thousands of well people, would not be smaller than the number of those who shall be cast out in suffering, compared with those who shall have upon them the health of heaven. For we are to remember that we are living in only the beginning of the Christian dispensation, and that this whole world is to be populated and redeemed, and that ages of light and love are to flow on. If this be so, the multitudes of the saved will be in vast majority. Take all the congregations that have assembled for worship throughout Christendom. Put them together, and they would make but a small audience compared with the thousands and tens of thousands, and ten thousand times ten thousands, and the hundred and forty and four thousand that shall stand around the throne. Those flashed up to heaven in martyr fires; those tossed for many years upon the invalid couch; those fought in the armies of liberty and rose as they fell; those tumbled from high scaffolding or slipped from the mast, or were washed off into the sea. They came up from Corinth, from Laodicea, from the Red Sea bank and Gennesaret's wave, from Egyptian brick-yards, and Gideon's threshing floor. Those thousands of years ago slept the last sleep, and these are this moment having their eyes closed, and their limbs stretched out for the sepulcher.

A general, expecting an attack from the enemy stands

on a hill and looks through a field glass, and sees, in the great distance, multitudes approaching, but has no idea of their numbers. He says: "I cannot tell anything about them. I merely know that there are a great number." And so John, without attempting to count, says: "A great multitude that no man can number." We are told that heaven is a place of happiness but what do we know about happiness? Happiness in this world is only a half fledged thing, flowery path, with a serpent hissing across it; a broken pitcher, from which the water has dropped before we could drink it; a thrill of exhilaration, followed by disastrous reactions. To help us understand the joy of heaven, the Bible takes us to a river. We stand on the grassy bank. We see the waters flow on with ceaseless wave. But the filth of the cities is emptied into it, and the banks are torn, and unhealthy exhalations spring up from it, and we fail to get an idea of the river of life in heaven.

A GLORIOUS AND EVERLASTING REUNION.

We get very imperfect ideas of the reunions of heaven. We think of some festal day on earth, when father and mother were yet living, and the children come home. A good time that! But it had this drawback—all were not there. That brother went off to sea, and never was heard from. That sister—did we not lay her away in the freshness of her young life, never more in this world to look upon her? Ah! there was a skeleton at the feast: and tears mingled with our laughter on that Christmas day. Not so with heaven's reunions. It will be an uninterrupted gladness. Many a Christian parent will look around and find all his children there. "Ah!" he says, "can it be possible that we are all here, life's perils over? The Jordan passed and not one wanting? Why, even the prodigal is here. I almost gave him up. How long he despised my counsels! but grace hath triumphed. All here! all here! Tell the mighty joy through the city. Let the bells ring, and the angels mention it in their song. Wave it from the top of the walls. All here!"

No more breaking of heart strings, but face to face. The orphans that were left poor, and in a merciless world, kicked and cuffed of many hardships, shall join their parents over whose graves they so long wept, and gaze into their glorified countenances forever, face to face. We may come up from different parts of the world, one from the land and another from the depths of the sea; from lives affluent and prosperous, or from scenes of ragged distress; but we shall all meet in rapture and jubilee, face to face.

Many of our friends have entered on that joy. A few days ago they sat with us studying these gospel themes; but they only saw dimly—now revelation hath come. Your time will also come. God will not leave you floundering in the darkness. You stand wonder struck and amazed. You feel as if all the loveliness of life were dashed out. You stand gazing into the open chasm of the grave. Wait a little. In the presence of your departed and of him who carries them in his bosom, you shall soon stand face to face. Oh! that our last hour may kindle up with this promised joy! May we be able to say, like the Christian not long ago, departing: "Though a pilgrim walking through the valley, the mountain tops are gleaming from peak to peak!" or, like my dear friend and brother, Alfred Cookman, who took his flight to the throne of God, saying in his last moment that which has already gone into Christian classics: "I am sweeping through the pearly gate, washed in the blood of the Lamb!"

UNFORGOTTEN.

IN JOPPA.

THE BELOVED DORCAS.

[Delivered in Joppa, Palestine, December 1st, 1889.]

"And all the widows stood by him weeping, and showing the coats and garments which Dorcas made while she was with them."
                                                    Acts ix, 39.

DORCAS, JUDAS MACCABAEUS AND NAPOLEON.

CHRISTIANS of Joppa! Impressed as I am with your mosque, the first I ever saw, and stirred as I am with the fact that your harbor once floated the great rafts of Lebanon cedar from which the temple at Jerusalem was builded, Solomon's oxen drawing the logs through this very town on the way to Jerusalem, nothing can make me forget that this Joppa was the birthplace of the sewing society that has blessed the poor of all succeeding ages in all lands. The disasters to your town when Judas Maccabæus set it on fire and Napoleon had 500 prisoners massacred in your neighborhood can not make me forget that one of the most magnificent charities of the centuries was started in this seaport by Dorcas, a woman with her needle embroidering her name ineffaceably into the beneficence of the world.

DORCAS HAS BEEN HERE—AN ELOQUENT TRIBUTE.

I see her sitting in yonder home. In the doorway, and around about the building, and in the room where she sits are the pale faces of the poor. She listens to their plaint, she pities their woe, she makes garments for them, she adjusts the manufactured articles to suit the bent form of this invalid woman and to the cripple that comes crawling on his hands and knees. She gives a coat to this one, she gives sandals to that one. With the gifts she mingles prayers and tears and Christian encouragement. Then she goes out to be greeted on the street corners by those whom she blessed and all through the street the cry is heard: "Dorcas is coming!" The sick look up gratefully in her face as she puts her hand on the burning brow, and the lost and the abandoned start up with hope as they hear her gentle voice, as though an angel had addressed them; and as she goes out the lane, eyes half put out with sin think they see a halo of light about her brow and a trail of glory in her pathway. That night a half-paid shipwright climbs the hill and reaches home and sees his little boy well clad and says: "Where did these clothes come from?" And they tell him, "Dorcas has been here." In another place a woman is trimming a lamp; Dorcas bought the oil. In another place a family that had not been at table for many a week are gathered now, for Dorcas has brought bread.

GREAT WEEPING IN JOPPA.

But there is a sudden pause in that woman's ministry. They say: Where is Dorcas? Why we haven't seen her for many a day? Where is Dorcas? And one of these poor people goes up and knocks at the door and finds the mystery solved! All through the haunts of wretchedness, the news comes "Dorcas is sick!" No bulletin flashing from the palace gate, telling the stages of a king's disease, is more anxiously awaited than the news from this sick benefactress. Alas! for Joppa! there is wailing, wailing. That voice which has uttered so many cheerful words is hushed; that hand which has made so many garments for the poor is cold and still; the star which has poured light into the midnight of wretchedness is dimmed by the blinding mists that go up from the river of death. In every God forsaken place in this town; wherever there is a sick child and no balm; wherever there is hunger and no bread; wherever there is guilt and no commiseration; wherever there is a broken heart and no comfort, there are despairing looks and streaming eyes, and frantic gesticulations as they cry: "Dorcas is dead!" They send for the apostle Peter, who happens to be in the suburbs of this place, stopping with a tanner by the name of Simon.

THE APOSTLE PETER APPEARS ON THE SCENE.

Peter urges his way through the crowd around the door and stands in the presence of the dead. What expostulation and grief all about him! Here stand some of the poor people, who show the garments which this poor woman had made for them. Their grief can not be appeased. The apostle Peter wants to perform a miracle. He will not do it amid the excited crowd, so he kindly orders that the whole room be cleared. The door is shut against the populace. The apostle stands now with the dead. Oh, it is a serious moment, you know, when you are alone with a lifeless body! The apostle gets down on his knees and prays, and then he comes to the lifeless form of this one all ready for the sepulcher and in the strength of him who is the resurrection he exclaims: "Tabitha, arise!" There is a stir in the fountains of life; the heart flutters; the nerves thrill; the cheek flushes; the eye opens; she sits up!

We see in this subject Dorcas the disciple, Dorcas the benefactress, Dorcas the lamented, Dorcas the resurrected.

DORCAS, THE DISCIPLE.

If I had seen that word disciple in my text I would have known this woman was a Christian. Such music as that never came from a heart which is not chorded and strung by divine grace. Before I show you the needlework of this woman I want to show you her regenerated heart, the source of a pure life and of all christian charities. I wish that the wives and mothers and daughters and sisters of all the earth would imitate Dorcas in her discipleship. Before you cross the threshold of the hospital, before you enter upon the temptations and trials of tomorrow, I charge you, in the name of God and by the turmoil and tumult of the judgment day, O women! that you attend to the first, last, and greatest duty of your life— the seeking for God and being at peace with him.

When the trumpet shall sound there will be an uproar, and a wreck of mountain and continent, and no human arm can help you. Amid the rising of the dead,

THE FLOOD.

and amid the boiling of yonder sea, and amid the live, leaping thunders of the flying heavens, calm and placid will be every woman's heart who hath put her trust in Christ; calm, notwithstanding all the tumult, as though the fire in the heavens were only the harmony of an orchestra, as though the awful voices of the sky were but a group of friends bursting through a gateway at eventime with laughter and shouting; "Dorcas, the disciple!" Would God that every Mary and every Martha would this day sit down at the feet of Jesus.

DORCAS, THE BENEFACTRESS.

Further, we see Dorcas the benefactress. History has told the story of the crown; the epic poet has sung of the sword; the pastoral poet, with his verses full of redolence of clover tops, and a-rustle with the silk of the corn, has sung the praises of the plow. I tell you the praises of the needle. From the fig leaf robe prepared in the garden of Eden to the last stitch taken on the garment for the poor, the needle has wrought wonders of kindness, generosity, and benefaction. It adorned the girdle of the high priest; it fashioned the curtains of the ancient tabernacle; it cushioned the chariots of King Solomon; it provided the robes of Queen Elizabeth; and in the high places and in the low places, by the fire of the pioneer's back log and under the flash of the chandelier, everywhere, it has clothed nakedness, it has preached the gospel, it has overcome hosts of penury and want with the war-cry of "Stitch, stitch, stitch!" The operatives have found a livelihood by it, and through it the mansions of the employer have been constructed. Amid the greatest triumphs of all ages and lands I set down the conquests of the needle. I admit its crimes; I admit its cruelties. It has had more martyrs than the fire, it has punctured the eye, it has pierced the side, it has stuck weakness in the lungs, it has sent madness into the brain, it has filled potter's field, it has pitched whole armies of the suffering into crime and wretchedness and woe. But now that I am talking of Dorcas and her ministries to the poor, I shall speak only of the charities of the needie.

This woman was a representative of all those women who make garments for the destitute, who knit socks for the barefooted, who prepare bandages for the lacerated, who fix up boxes of clothing for missionaries, who go into the asylums of the suffering and destitute bearing that gospel which is sight for the blind and hearing for the deaf, and which makes the lame man leap like a hart and brings the dead to life, immortal health bounding in their pulses. What a contrast between the practical benevolence of this woman and a great deal of the charity of this day! This woman did not spend her time idly planning how the poor of your city of Joppa were to be relieved; she took her needle and relieved them. She was not like those persons who sympathize with imaginary sorrows and go out in the street and laugh at the boy who has upset his basket of cold vituals, or like that charity which makes a rousing speech on the benevolent platform, and goes out to kick the beggar from the step, crying: "Hush your miserable howling!"

The sufferers of the world want not so much theory as practice; not so much kind wishes as loaves of bread; not so much smiles as shoes; not so much "God bless yous!" as jackets and frocks. I will put one earnest Christian man, hard working, against 5,000 mere theorists on the subject of charity. There are a great many who have fine ideas about church architecture who never in their life helped to build a church. There are men who can give you the history of Buddhism and Mohammedanism who never sent a farthing for their evangelization. There are women who talk beautifully about the suffering of the world who never had the courage, like Dorcas, to take the needle and assault it.

QUEEN BLANCHE, QUEEN MAUD AND OTHER BENEFACTRESSES.

I am glad that there is not a page of the world's history which is not a record of female benevolence. God says to all lands and people, Come now and hear the widow's mite rattle down into the poor box. The princess of Counti sold all her jewels that she might help the famine-stricken. Queen Blanche, the wife of Louis VIII. of France, hearing that there were some persons unjustly incarcerated in the prisons, went out amidst the rabble and took a stick and struck the door as a signal that they might all strike it, and down went the prison door, and out came the prisoners. Queen Maud, the wife of Henry I., went down amidst the poor and washed their sores and administered to them cordials. Mrs. Retson, at Matagorda, appeared on the battle-field while the missiles of death were flying around, and cared for the wounded. Is there a man or woman who has ever heard of the civil war in America who has not heard of the women of the sanitary and Christian commissions, or the fact that before the smoke had gone up from Gettysburg and South Mountain the women of the north met the women of south on the battle-field, forgetting all their animosities while they bound up the wounded and closed the eyes of the slain? Dorcas the benefactress.

I come now to speak of Dorcas the lamented. When

MARY AND MARTHA.

death struck down that good woman, oh, how much sorrow there was in this town of Joppa! I suppose there were women here with larger fortunes; women, perhaps, with handsomer faces; but there was no grief at their departure like this at the death of Dorcas. There was not more turmoil and upturning in the Mediterranean sea, dashing against the wharves of this seaport, then there were surgings to and fro of grief because Dorcas was dead. There are a great many who go out of life and are unmissed. There may be a very large funeral; there may be a great many carriages and a plumed hearse; there may be high-sounding eulogiums; the bell may toll at the cemetery gate; there may be a very fine marble shaft reared over the resting place; but the whole thing may be a false-hood and a sham. The church of God has lost nothing, the world has lost nothing. It is only a nuisance abated; it is only a grumbler ceasing to find fault; it is only an idler stopped yawning; it is only a dissipated fashionable, parted from his wine cellar; while, on the other hand, no useful Christian leaves this world without being missed. The church of God cries out like the prophet: "Howl, fir tree, for the cedar has fallen." Widowhood comes and shows the garments which the departed had made. Orphans are lifted up to look into the calm face of the sleeping benefactress. Reclaimed vagrancy comes and kisses the cold brow of her who charmed it away from sin, and all through the streets of Joppa there is mourning—mourning because Dorcas is dead.

BURIAL OF JOSEPHINE OF FRANCE.

When Josephine of France was carried out to her grave there were a great many men and women of pomp and pride and position that went out after her;

but I am most affected by the story of history that on that day there were 10,000 of the poor of France who followed her coffin, weeping and wailing until the air rang again, because when they lost Josephine they lost their last earthly friend. Oh, who would not rather have such obsequies than all the tears that were ever poured in the lachrymals that have been exhumed from ancient cities. There may be no mass for the dead; there may be no costly sacrophagus; there may be no elaborate mausoleum; but in the damp cellars of the city and through the lonely huts of the mountain glen there will be mourning, mourning, mourning, because Dorcas is dead. "Blessed are the dead who die in the Lord; they rest from their labors and their works do follow them."

I speak to you of Dorcas the resurrected. The apostle came to where she was and said: "Arise; and she sat up!" In what a short compass the writer put that— "She sat up!" Oh, what a time there must have been around this town when the apostle brought her out among her old friends! How the tears of joy must have started! What clapping of hands there must have been! What singing! What laughter! Sound it all through that lane! Shout it down that dark alley! Let all Joppa hear it! Dorcas is resurrected!

You and I have seen the same thing many a time; not a dead body resuscitated, but the deceased coming up again after death in the good accomplished. If a man labors up to fifty years of age, serving God, and then dies, we are apt to think that his earthly work is done. No. His influence on earth will continue till the world ceases. Services rendered for Christ never stops. A Christian woman toils for the upbuilding of a church through many anxieties, through many self denials, with prayers and tears, and then she dies. It is fifteen years since she went away. Now the spirit of God descends upon the church; hundreds of souls stand up and confess the faith in Christ. Has that Christian woman who went away fifteen years ago nothing to do with these things? I see the flowering out of her noble heart. I hear the echo of her footsteps in all the songs over sin forgiven, in all the prosperity of the church. The good that seemed to be buried has come up again. Dorcas is resurrected.

After awhile all these womanly friends of Christ will put down their needles forever. After making garments for others some one will make a garment for them; the last robe we ever wear—the robe for the grave. You will have heard the last cry of pain. You will have witnessed the last orphanage. You will have come in worn out from your last round of mercy. I do not know where you will sleep nor what your epitaph will be; but there will be a lamp burning at that tomb and an angel of God guarding it, and through all the long night no rude foot will disturb the dust. Sleep on, sleep on! Soft bed, pleasant shadows, undisturbed repose! Sleep on!

    Asleep in Jesus! Blessed sleep!
    From which none ever wakes to weep.

Then one day there will be a sky rending, and a whirl of wheels, and the flash of a pageant; armies marching, chains clanking, banners waving, thunders booming, and that Christian woman will arise from the dust, and she will be suddenly surrounded—surrounded by the wanderers of the street whom she reclaimed, surrounded by the wounded souls to whom she had administered! Daughter of God, so strangely surrounded, what means this! It means that reward has come, that the victory is won, that the crown is ready, that the banquet is spread. Shout it through all the crumbling earth.

Sing it through all the flying heavens. Dorcas is resurrected.

A STORY OF THE QUEEN OF ENGLAND.

In 1885, when some of the soldiers came back from the Crimean war to London, the Queen of England distributed among them beautiful medals, called Crimean medals. Galleries were erected for the two houses of parliament and the royal family to sit in. There was a great audience to witness the distribution of the medals. A colonel who had lost both feet in the battle of Inkerman was pulled in on a wheel-chair; others came in limping on their crutches. Then the queen of England arose before them in the name of the government and uttered words of commendation to the officers and men and distributed these medals, inscribed with the four great battlefields—Alma, Balaklava, Inkerman, and Sebastopol. As the queen gave these to the wounded men and the wounded officers the bands of music struck up the national air and the people with streaming eyes joined in the song:

> God save our gracious queen!
> Long live our noble queen!
> God save the queen!

And then they shouted, "Huzzah! huzzah!" Oh, it was a proud day for those returned warriors!

But a brighter, better, and gladder day will come when Christ shall gather those who have toiled in his service, good soldiers of Jesus Christ. He shall rise before them, and in the presence of all the glorified of heaven he will say: "Well done, good and faithful servant!" and then he will distribute the medals of eternal victory, not inscribed with works of righteousness which we have done, but with those four great battlefields, dear to earth and dear to heaven, Bethlehem! Nazareth! Gethsemane! Calvary!

THE HOLY CITY.

THE GOLDEN AGE OF JERUSALEM.
[Delivered in Jerusalem, December 8, 1889.]

"Jerusalem! Jerusalem!" Matt. xxiii, 37.

JERUSALEM! JERUSALEM!—ITS MIGHTY PAST.

THIS exclamation burst from Christ's lips as He came in sight of this great city, and although things have marvelously changed, who can visit Jerusalem to-day without having its mighty past roll over on him, and ordinary utterance must give place for the exclamatory as we cry, O, Jerusalem, Jerusalem! Disappointed with the Holy Land many have been,

(75)

and I have heard good friends say that their ardor about sacred places had been so dampened that they were sorry they ever visited Jerusalem. But with me the city and its surroundings are a rapture, a solemnity an overwhelming emotion. O! Jerusalem, Jerusalem! The procession of kings, conquerors, poets and immortal men and women pass before me as I stand here. Among the throng are Solomon David and Christ.

SOLOMON'S SPLENDOR PORTRAYED.

Yes, through these streets and amid these surroundings rode Solomon, that wonder of splendor and wretchedness. It seemed as if the world exhausted itself on that man. It wove its brightest flowers into his garland. It set its richest gems in his coronet. It pressed the rarest wine to his lips. It robed him in the purest purple and embroidery. It cheered him with the sweetest music in that land of harps. It greeted him with the gladdest laughter that ever leaped from mirth's lip. It sprinkled his cheek with spray from the brightest fountains. Royalty had no dominion, wealth no luxury, gold no glitter, flowers no sweetness, song no melody, light no radiance, upholstery no gorgeousness, waters no gleam, birds no plumage, prancing coursers no mettle, architecture no grandeur but it was all his. Across the thick grass of the lawn, fragrant with tufts of camphire from Engedi, fell the long shadows of trees brought from distant forests.

Fish pools, fed by artificial channels that brought the streams from hills far away, were perpetually ruffled with fins, and golden scales shot from water cave to water cave with endless dive swirl, attracting the gaze of foreign potentates. Birds that had been brought from foreign aviaries glanced and fluttered among the foliage, and called to their mates far beyond the sea. From the royal stables there came up the neighing of twelve thousand horses, standing in blankets of Tyrian purple, chewing their bits over troughs of gold, waiting for the king's order to be brought out in front of the palace when the official dignitaries would leap into the saddle for some grand parade, or harnessed to some of the fourteen hundred chariots of the king, the fiery chargers with flaunting mane and throbbing nostril would make the earth jar with the tramp of hoofs and the thunder of wheels. While within and without the palace you could not think of a single luxury that could be added, or of a single splendor that could be kindled, down on the banks of the sea the dry docks of Ezion-geber rang with the hammers of the shipwrights who were constructing larger vessels for a still wider commerce, for all lands and climes were to be robbed to make up Solomon's glory. No rest till his keels shall cut every sea, his axmen hew every forest, his archers strike every rare wing, his fishermen whip every stream, his merchants trade in every bazaar, his name be honored by every tribe; and royalty shall have no dominion, wealth no luxury, gold no glitter, song no melody, light no radiance, waters no gleam, birds no plumage, prancing coursers no mettle, upholstery no gorgeousness, architecture no grandeur, but it was all his.

BUT SOLOMON IS NOT HAPPY.

"Well," you say, "if there is any man happy, he ought to be." But I hear him coming out through the palace, and see his robes actually incrusted with jewels, as he stands in the front and looks out upon the vast domain. What does he say? King Solomon, great is your dominion, great is your honor, great is your joy? No. While standing here amidst all the splendor, the tears start, and his heart breaks and he exclaims: "Vanity of vanities; all is vanity." What! Solomon not happy yet? No, not happy. The honors and the emoluments of this world brings as many cares with them that they bring also torture and disquietude. Pharoah sits on one of the highest earthly eminences, yet he is miserable because there are some people in his realm that do not want any longer to make bricks. The head of Edward I. aches under his crown because the people will not pay the taxes, and Llewellyn, Prince of Wales, will not do him homage, and Wallace will be a hero. Frederick William III, of Prussia, is miserable because France wants to take the Prussian Provinces. The world is not large enough for Louis XIV and Willian III. The ghastliest suffering, the most shriveling fear, the most rendering jealousies, the most gigantic disquietude, have walked amidst obsequious courtiers, and been clothed in royal apparel, and sat on judgment seats of power.

Honor and truth and justice cannot go so high up in authority as to be beyond the range of human assault. The pure and good in all ages have been execrated by the mob who cry out: "Not this man, but Barabbas. Now, Barabbas was a robber." By honesty, by Christian principle, I would have you seek for the favor and the confidence of your fellow men; but do not look upon some high position as though that were always sunshine. The mountains of earthly honor are like the mountains of Switzerland, covered with perpetual ice and snow. Having obtained the confidence and love of your associates, be content with such things as you have. You brought nothing into the world, and it is very certain you can carry nothing out. "Cease ye from man, whose breath is in his nostrils." There is an honor that is worth possessing, but it is an honor that comes from God. This day rise up and take it. "Behold what manner of love the father hath bestowed upon us, that we should be called the sons of God." Who aspires not for that royalty? Come now, and be kings and priests unto God and the lamb forever.

If wealth and wisdom could have satisfied a man, Solomon would have been satisfied. To say that Solomon was a millionaire gives but a very imperfect idea of the property he inherited from David, his father.

SOLOMON'S RICHES, WISDOM AND WRETCHEDNESS.

He had at his command gold to the value of six hundred and eighty millon pounds, and he had silver to the value of one billion, twenty-nine million, three hundred and seventy-seven pounds sterling. The queen of Sheba made him a nice little present of seven hundred and twenty thousand pounds, and Hiram made him a present of the same amount. If he had lost the value of a whole realm out of his pocket, it would hardly have been worth his while to stoop down and pick it up. He wrote one thousand and five songs. He wrote three thousand proverbs. He wrote about almost everything. The Bible says distinctly he wrote about plants, from the cedar of Lebanon to the hyssop that groweth out of the wall, and about birds and beasts and fishes. No doubt he put off his royal robes, and put on hunter's trapping, and went out with his arrows to bring down the rarest specimens of birds; and then with his fishing apparatus he went down to the stream to bring up the denizens of the deep, and plunged into the forest and found the rarest specimens of flowers and then he came back to his study and wrote books about zoology, the science of animals; about ichthyology, the science of fishes; about ornithology, the science of birds; about botany, the science of plants. Yet, notwithstanding all his wisdom and wealth, behold his wretchedness, and let him pass on. Did any other city ever behold so wonderful a man? O Jerusalem, Jerusalem!

THE CITY OF DAVID—SORROW FOR ABSALOM.

But here passes through these streets, as in imagination I see him, quite as wonderful and a far better man. David the conqueror, the king, the poet. Can it be that I am in the very city where he lived and reigned! David great for power, and great for grief. He was wrapped up in his boy Absalom. He was a splendid boy, judged by the rules of worldly criticism. From the crown of his head to the sole of his foot there was not a single blemish. The Bible says that he had such a luxuriant shock of hair that, when once a year it was shorn, what was cut off weighed over three pounds. But, notwithstanding all his brilliancy of appearance, he was a bad boy, and broke his father's heart. He was plotting to get the throne of Israel. He had marshalled an army to overthrow his father's government. The day of battle had come. The conflict was begun. David, the father, sat between the gates of the palace waiting for the tidings of the conflict. Oh, how rapidly his heart beat with emotion! Two great questions were to be decided; the safety of his boy, and the continuance of the throne of Israel. After awhile, a servant, standing on the top of the house, looks off, and he sees some one running. He is coming with great speed, and the man on top of the house announces the coming of the messenger, and the father watches and waits, and

OH, JERUSALEM! JERUSALEM!

as soon as the messenger from the field of battle comes within hailing distance the father cries out. Is it a question in regard to the establishment of his throne? Does he say: "Have the armies of Israel been victorious? Am I to continue in my imperial authority? Have I overthrown my enemies?" Oh, no. There is one question that springs from his heart to his lip, and springs from the lip into the ear of the besweated and bedusted messenger flying from the battlefield—the question: "Is the young man Absalom safe!" When it was told to David, the king, that, though his armies had been victorious, his son had been slain, the father turned his back upon the congratulations of the nation, and went up the stairs of his palace, his heart breaking as he went, wringing his hands sometimes, and then again pressing them against his temples as though he would press them in, crying: "O Absalom! my son! my son! Would God I had died for thee, O Absalom! my son! my son!" Stupendous grief of David resounding through all succeeding ages. This was the city that heard the woe. O Jerusalem, Jerusalem!

THE CITY OF GREAT TEMPLES.

I am also thrilled and overpowered with the remembrance that yonder, where now stands a Mohammedan mosque, stood the temple, the very one that Christ visited. Solomon's temple had stood there, but Nebuchadnezzar thundered it down. Zerubbabel's temple had stood there, but that had been prostrated! Then Herod built a temple because he was fond of great architecture, and he wanted the preceding temples to seem insignificant. Put eight or ten modern cathedrals together, and they would not equal that structure. It covered nineteen acres. There were marble pillars supporting roofs of cedar, and silver tables on which stood golden cups, and there were carvings exquisite and inscriptions resplendent, glittering balustrades and ornamented gateways. The building of this temple kept ten thousand workmen busy forty-six years. Stupendous pile of pomp and magnificence! But the material and architectural grandeur of the building were very tame compared with the spiritual meaning of its altars and holy of holies, and the overwhelming significance of its ceremonies. O Jerusalem, Jerusalem!

CHRIST'S TRIUMPHAL ENTRY.

But standing in this old city all other facts are eclipsed when we think that near here our blessed Lord was born, that up and down the streets of this city he walked, and that in the outskirts of it he died. Here was his only day of trimph and his assassination. One day this old Jerusalem is at the tiptop of excitement. Christ has been doing some remarkable works and asserting very high authority. The police court has issued papers for his arrest; for this thing must be stopped, as the very government is imperiled. News comes that last night this stranger arrived at a suburban village and that he is stopping at the house of a man whom he had resuscitated after four days sepulture. Well, the people rush out into the streets, some with the idea of helping in the arrest of this stranger when he arrives, and others expecting that on the morrow he will come into the town and by some supernatural force oust the municipal and royal authorities and take everything in his own hands. They pour out of the city gates until the procession reaches to the village. They come all around about the house where the stranger is stopping, and peer into the doors and windows that they may get one glimpse of him or hear the hum of his voice. The police dare not make the arrest, because he has

THE ROYAL RIDE INTO JERUSALEM.

somehow won the affections of all the people. Oh; it is a lively night in yonder Bethany! The heretofore quiet village is filled with uproar. and outcry and loud discussion about the strange acting countryman. I do not think there was any sleep in that house that night where the stranger was stopping. Although he came in weary he finds no rest, though for once in his lifetime he had a pillow. But the morning dawns, the olive gardens wave in the light, all along yonder road, reaching the top of Olive. toward this city, there is a vast swaying crowd of wondering people. The excitement around the door of the cottage is wild as the stranger steps out besides an unbroken colt that had never been mounted, and after his friends had strewn their garments on the beast for a saddle the Saviour mounts it, and the populace, excited and shouting and feverish, push on back toward this city of Jerusalem.

"HOSANNA! HOSANNA!" CRY THE PEOPLE.

Let none jeer now or scoff at this rider; or the populace will trample him under foot in an instant. There is one long shout of two miles, and as far as the eye can reach you see wavings of demonstrations and approval. There was something in the rider's visage, something in his majestic brow, something in his princely behavior, that stirs up the enthusiasm of the people. They run up against the beast and try to pull the rider off into their arms and carry on their shoulders the illustrious stranger. The populace are so excited that they hardly know what to do with themselves, and some rush up to the roadside trees and wrench off branches and throw them in his way; and others doff their garments, what though they be new and costly, and spread them for a carpet for the conquerer to ride over. "Hosanna!" cry the people at the foot of the hill. "Hosanna!" cry the people all up and down the mountain.

THE SCENE FROM OLIVET.

The procession has now come to the brow of yonder Olivet. Magnificent prospect reaching out in every direction—vineyards, olive groves, jutting rock, silvery Siloam, and above all, rising on its throne of hills, this most highly honored city of all the earth, Jerusalem. Christ there, in the midst of the procession, looks off and sees here fortressed gates, and yonder the circling wall, and here the towers blazing in the sun, Phasaelus and Mariamme. Yonder is Hippicus, the king's castle. Looking along in the range of the larger branch of that olive tree, you see the mansions of the merchant princes. Through this cleft in the limestone rock you see the palace of the richest trafficker in all the earth. He has made his money by selling Tyrian purple. Behold now the temple! Clouds of smoke lifting from the shimmering roof, while the building rises up beautiful, grand, majestic, the architectural skill and glory of the earth lifting themselves there in one triumphant doxology, the frozen prayer of all nations. The crowd looked around to see exhilaration and transport in the face of Christ. Oh, no! Out from amid the gates, and the domes, and the palaces, there arose a vision of the city's sin, and of this citiy's doom, which obliterated the landscape from horizon to horizon, and he burst into tears, crying; "O Jerusalem, Jerusalem!" But that was the only day of pomp that Jesus saw in and around this city. Yet he walked the streets of this city the lovliest and most majestic being that the world ever saw or ever will see.

A ROMAN LETTER DESCRIBING JESUS.

Publius Lentilus, in a letter to the Roman senate, de-

THE MOUNT OF OLIVES.

scribes him as "a man of stature somewhat tall, his hair the color of a chestnut fully ripe, plain to the ears, whence downward it is more orient, curling and waving about the shoulders; in the midst of his forehead is a stream, or partition of his hair; forehead plain, and very delicate: his face without a spot or a wrinkle, a lovely red; his nose and mouth so forked as nothing can be represented; his beard thick, in color like his hair—not very long; his eyes gray, quick and clear."

THE CITY OF CHRIST'S AGONY AND DEATH!

He must die. The French army in Italy found a brass plate on which was a copy of his death warrant, signed by John Ferubbabel, Raphael Robani, Daniel Roban and Capet. Sometimes men on the way to the scaffold have been rescued by the mob. No such attempt was made in this case, for the mob were against him. From nine in the morning, until three in the afternoon, Jesus hung a-dying in the outskirts of this city. It was the scene of blood. We are so constituted that nothing is so exciting as blood. It is not the child's cry in the street that arouses you as the crimson dripping from his lip. In the dark hall, seeing the finger marks of blood on the plastering, you cry: "What terrible deed has been done here?" Looking upon this suspended victim of the cross, we thrill with the sight of blood—blood dripping from thorn and nail, blood rushing upon his cheek, blood saturating his garments, blood gathered in a pool beneath. It is called an honor to have in one's veins the blood of the house of Stuart, or of the house of Hapsburg. Is it nothing when I point you to the outpouring blood of the king of the universe?

In England the name of Henry was so great that its

honors were divided among different reigns. It was Henry the First, and Henry the Second, and Henry the Third, and Henry the Fourth, and Henry the Fifth. In France the name of Louis was so favorably regarded that it was Louis the First, Louis the Second, Louis the Third, and so on. But the king who walked these streets was Christ the First, and Christ the Last, and Christ the Only. He reigned before the czar mounted the throne of Russia, or the throne of Austria was titled, "king eternal, immortal." Through indulgences of the royal family, the physical life degenerates, and some of the kings have been almost imbecile, and their bodies weak, and their blood thin and watery: But the crimson life that flowed upon Calvary had in it the health of immortal God.

THE LAST SAD HOUR.

Tell it now to all the earth, and to all the heavens—Jesus, our king, is sick with his last sickness. Let couriers carry the swift dispach. His pains are worst; he is breathing a last groan; through his body quivers the last anguish; the king is dying; the king is dead!

It is royal blood. It is said that some religionists make too much of the humanity of Christ. I respond that we make too little. If some Roman surgeon, standing under the cross, had caught one drop of the blood on his hand and analyzed it, it wonld have been found to have the same plasma, the same disk, the same fibrin, the same albumen. It was unmistakably human blood. It is a man that hangs there. His bones are of the same material as ours. If it were an angel being despoiled I would not feel it so much, for it belongs to a different order of beings. But my Savoir is a man, and my whole sympathy is aroused. I can imagine how the spikes felt—how hot the temples burned—what deadly sickness seized his heart—how mountain, and city, and mob swam away from his dying vision—something of the meaning of that cry for help that makes the blood of all the ages curdle with horror: "My God! my God! why hast thou forsaken me?"

Forever with all these scenes of a Savior's suffering will this city be associeted. Here his unjust trial and here his death. O Jerusalem, Jerusalem!

THE NEW JERUSALEM.

But finally I am thrilled with the fact that this city is a symbol of heaven which is only another Jerusalem. "The New Jerusalem!" And this thought has kindled the imagination of all the sacred poets. I am glad that Horatio Bonar the Scotch hymnist rummaged among old manuscripts of the British museum until he found that hymn in ancient spelling, parts of which we have in mutilated form in our modern hymn books, but the quaint power of which we do not get in our modern versions:

> Hierusalem, my happy home!
> When shall I come to thee?
> When shall my sorrows have an end,
> Thy joys when shall I see?
>
> Noe dampish mist is seene in thee,
> Noe colde nor darksome night:
> There everie soule shines as the sunne,
> There God himselfe gives light.
>
> Thy walls are made of peetious stones,
> Thy bulwarkes diamondes square;
> Thy gates are of right orient pearle,
> Exceedinge riche and rare,
>
> Thy turrettes and thy pinnacles
> With carbuncles doe shine;
> Thy verrie streets are paved with gould,
> Surpassinge cleare and fine.

THE GOLDEN AGE.

Thy houses are of yvorie,
  Thy windows crystal cleare;
Thy tyles are made of beaten gould,
  O God! that I were there.

Our sweete is mixt with bittergaule,
  Our pleasure is but paine;
Our joyes scarce last the lookeing on.
  Our sorrowes stille remaine.

But there they live in such delight,
  Such pleasures and such play,
As that to them a thousand yeares
  Doth seem as yesterday.

Thy gardens and thy gallant walkes
  Continually are greene;
There grow such sweete and pleasant flowers
  As no where else are seene.

There trees for evermore beare fruite
  And evermore doe springe;
There evermore the angels sit,
  And evermore doe singe.

Hierusalem! my happie home!
  Would God I were in thee!
Would God my woes were at an end,
  Thy joyese that I might see!

JESUS CROSSING GALILEE, AND STILLING THE TEMPEST.

IN CAPERNAUM.

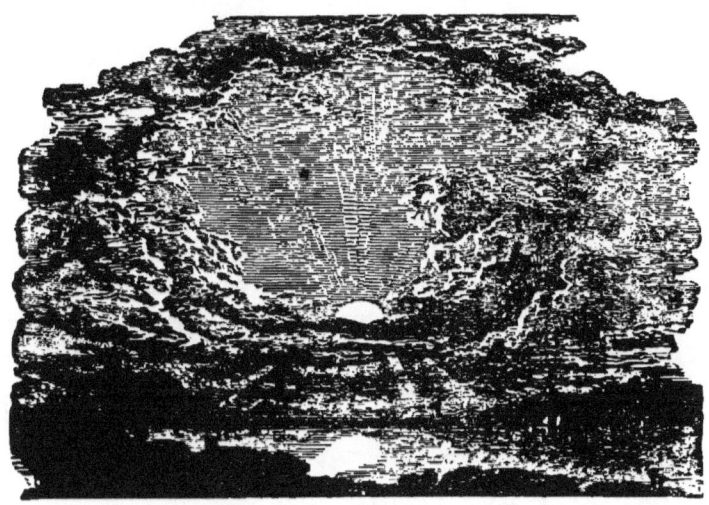

THE STORMY PASSAGE ON GALILEE.
[Delivered in Capernaum, Palestine, December, 15, 1890.]

"*And entered into a ship, and went over the sea toward Capernaum.*" *John vi, 17.*

"*And He arose and rebuked the wind.*" *Mark iv:39*

ON THE BANKS OF GALILEE.

HERE in this seashore village was the temporary home of that Christ who for the most of his life was homeless. On the site of this village, now in ruins, and all around this lake, what scenes of kindness, and power, and glory, and pathos when our Lord lived here! It has been the wish of my life—I cannot say the hope, for I never expected the privilege—to stand on the banks of Galilee. What a solemnity and what a rapture to be here! I can now understand the feeling of the immortal Scotchman, Robert McCheyne, when, sitting on the banks of this lake, he wrote:

(93)

"It is not that the wild gazelle
   Comes down to drink thy tide,
But he that was pierced to save from hell
   Oft wandered by thy side.
Graceful around thee the mountains meet,
   Thou calm reposing sea;
But ah! far more, the beautiful feet
   Of Jesus walked o'er thee."

I can now easily understand from the contour of the country that bounds this lake that storms were easily tempted to make these waters their play-ground. From the gentle way this lake treated our boats when we sailed on it yesterday one would have thought it incapable of a paroxysm of rage, but it was quite different on both the occasions spoken of in my two texts.

A BEAUTIFUL SCENE.

I close my eyes, and the shore of Lake Galilee as it now is, with but little signs of human life, disappears, and there comes back to my vision the lake as it was in Christ's time. It lay in a sense of great luxuriance; the surrounding hills, terraced, sloped, grooved, so many hanging gardens of beauty. On the shore were castles, armed towers, Roman baths, everything attractive and beautiful—all styles of vegetation in shorter space than in almost any other space in all the world, from the palm-tree of the forest, to the trees of rigorous climate.

It seemed as if the Lord had launched one wave of beauty on all the scene, and it hung and swung from rock and hill and oleander. Roman gentlemen in pleasure-boats sailing this lake and countrymen in fish-smacks coming down to drop their nets pass each other with nod, and shout, and laughter, or swinging idly at their mooring. Oh, what a beautiful scene! It seems as if we shall have a quiet night. Not a leaf winked in the air; not a ripple disturbed the face of Gennesaret, but there seems to be a little excitement up the beach and we hasten to see what it is and we find it is an embarkation.

ON THE SEA WITH CHRIST.

From the western shore a flotilla pushed out; not a squadron, or deadly armament, nor clipper with valuable merchandise, nor piratic vessel ready to destroy everything they could seize, but a flotilla bearing messengers of light, and life, and peace. Christ is in the front of the boat. His disciples are in a smaller boat. Jesus, weary with much speaking to large multitudes, is put into somnolence by the rocking of the waves. If there was any motion at all the ship was easily righted; if the wind passed from starboard to larboard or from larboard to starboard the boat would rock, and by the gentleness of the motion putting the master asleep. And they extemporized a pillow made out of a fisherman's coat. I think no sooner is Christ prostrate and his head touched the pillow than he is sound asleep. The breezes of the lake run their fingers through the locks of the worn sleeper and the boat rises and falls like a sleeping child on the bosom of a sleeping mother.

Calm night, starry night, beautiful night. Run up all the sails, ply all the oars, and let the large boat and the small boat glide over the gentle Gennesaret. But the sailors say there is going to be a change of weather. And even the passengers can hear the moaning of the storm as it comes on with great stride and all the terrors of hurricane and darkness. The large boat trembles like a deer at bay among the clangor of the hounds; great patches of foam are flung into the air; the sails of the vessel loosen, and the sharp winds crack like pistols; the smaller boats like petrels poise on the cliffs of the waves and then plunge.

CHRIST STILLING THE TEMPEST.

Overboard go cargo, tackling, and masts, and the drenched disciples rush into the back part of the boat and lay hold of Christ and say unto him; "Master carest thou not that we perish?" That great personage lifts his head from the pillow of the fisherman's coat, walks to the front of the vessel, and looks out into the storm. All around him are the smaller boats, driven in the tempest, and through it comes the cry of drowning men. By the flash of the lightning I see the calm brow of Christ as the spray dropped from his beard. He has one word for the sky and another for the waves. Looking upward he cries: "Peace!" Looking downward he says: "Be still!"

The waves fall flat on their faces, the foam melts, the extinguished stars relight their torches. The tempest falls dead and Christ stands with his feet on the neck of the storm. And while the sailors are bailing out the boats, and while they are trying to untangle the cordage the disciples stand in amazement, now looking into the calm sea, then into the calm sky, then into the calm Savior's countenance, and they cry out: "What manner of a man is this that even the winds and the sea obey him?"

HAVE CHRIST ON YOUR SHIP

The subject in the first place impresses me with the fact that it is very important to have Christ in the ship, for all those boats would have gone to the bottom of Gennesaret if Christ had not been present. Oh, what a lesson for you and for me to learn! We must always

have Christ in the ship. Whatever voyage we undertake, into whatever enterprise we start, let us always have Christ in the ship. All you can do with utmost tension of body, and mind, and soul you are bound to do, but oh! have Christ in every enterprise, Christ in every voyage.

There are men who ask God's help at the beginning of great enterprises. He has been with them in the past; no trouble can overthrow them; the storms might come down from the top of mount Hermon and lash Gennesaret into foam and into agony, but it could not hurt them. But here is another man who starts out in worldly enterprise, and he depends on the uncertainties of this life. He has no God to help him. After awhile the storm comes and tosses off the masts of the ship; he puts out his life-boat and the long boat; the sheriff and the auctioneer try to help him off; they can't help him off; he must go down—no Christ in the ship. Your life will be made up of sunshine and shadows. There may be in it Arctic blasts or tropical tornadoes; I know not what is before you, but I know if you have Christ with you all shall be well. You may seem to get along without the religion of Christ while everything goes smoothly, but after awhile, when sorrow hovers over the soul, when the waves of trial dash clear over the hurricane deck, and the decks are crowded with piratical disasters—oh, what would you do then without Christ in the ship? Take God for your portion, God for your guide, God for your help; then all is well; all is well for time, all shall be well forever. Blessed is that man who puts in the Lord his trust. He shall never be confounded.

But my subject also impresses me with the fact that **when** people start to follow Christ they must not

THE MARTYRS.

expect smooth sailing.

These disciples got into the small boats, and I have no doubt they said: "What a beautiful day this is! What a smooth sea! What a bright sky this is! How delightful is sailing in this boat! And as for the waves under the keel of the boat, why, they only make the motion of our little boat the more delightful." But when the winds swept down and the sea was tossed into wrath, then they found that following Christ was not smooth sailing. So you have found it; so I have found it. Did you ever notice the end of the life of the apostles of Jesus Christ? You would say, if ever men ought to have had a smooth life, a smooth departure, then those men, the disciples of Jesus Christ, ought to have had such a departure and such a life. St. James lost his head. St. Philip was hanged to death on a pillar. St. Matthew had his life dashed out with a halbert. St. Mark was dragged to death through the streets. St. James the Less was beaten to death with a fuller's club. St. Thomas was struck through with a spear. They did not find following Christ smooth sailing. Oh, how they were all tossed in the tempest! John Huss in the fire, Hugh McKall in the hour of martyrdom, the Albigenses, the Waldenses, the Scotch Covenanters—did they find it smooth sailing? But why go into history when we can draw from our own memory illustrations of the truth of what I say? Some young man in a store trying to serve God, while his employer scoffs at Christianity; the young men in the same store, antagonistic to the Christian religion, teasing him, tormenting him about his religion, trying to get him mad. They succeed in getting him mad, saying: "You'er a pretty Christian!" Does that young man find it smooth sailing when he tries to follow Christ? Or you remember a Christian girl. Her father despises the Christian religion; her mother despises the Christian religion; her brothers and sisters scoff at the Christian religion; she can hardly find a quiet place in which to say her prayers. Did she find it smooth sailing when she tried to follow Jesus Christ? Oh, no! All who would live the life of the Christian religion must suffer presecution: if you do not find it in one way you will get it in another way. The question was asked: "Who are the nearest the throne?" And the answer came back: "These are they who came up out of great tribulation—great flailing as the original has it; great flailing, great pounding—and had their robes washed and made white in the blood of the lamb." Oh, do not be disheartened! Take courage. You are in glorious companionship. God will see you through all trials and he will deliver you.

DO NOT BE FRIGHTENED.

My subject impresses me with the fact that good people sometimes get very much frightened.

In the tones of these disciples as they rushed into the back part of the boat I find they are frightened almost to death. They say: "Master, carest thou not that we perish?" They had no reason to be frightened, for Christ was in the boat. I suppose if we had been there we would have been just as much affrighted. Perhaps more. In all ages very good people get very much affrighted. It is often so in our day and men say: "Why, look at the bad lectures; look at the various errors going over the church of God. We are going to founder. The church is going to perish. She is going down." Oh, how many good people are affrighted by iniquity in our day and think the church of Jesus Christ is go-

ing to be overthrown, and are just as much affrighted as were the disciples of my text. Don't worry, don't fret, as though iniquity were going to triumph over righteousness. A lion goes into a cavern to sleep. He lies down, with his shaggy mane covering the paws. Meanwhile the spiders spin a web across the mouth of the cavern and say: "We have captured him." Gossamer thread after gossamer thread, until the whole front of the cavern is covered with the spiders' web and the spiders say: "The lion is done; the lion is fast." After awhile the lion has got through sleeping; he rouses himself; he shakes his mane; he walks out into the sunlight; he does not even know the spiders web is spun, and with his voice shakes the mountain. So men come spinning their sophistries and skepticism about Jesus Christ; he seems to be sleeping. They say: "We have captured the Lord; he will never come forth again upon the nation; Christ is captured forever. His religion will never make any conquest among men." But after awhile the lion of the tribe of Judah will rouse himself and come forth to shake mightily the nations. What's a spider's web to the aroused lion! Give truth and error a fair grapple and truth will come off victor.

But there are a great many good people who get affrighted in other respects; they are affrighted in our day about revivals. They say: "Oh! this is a strong religious gale; we are afraid the church of God is going to be upset, and there are going to be a great many people brought into the church that are going to be of no use to it," and they are affrighted whenever they see a revival taking hold of the churches. As though a ship captain, with 5,000 bushels of wheat for a cargo, should say some day, coming upon deck: "Throw overboard all the cargo," and the sailors should say: "Why, captain, what do you mean? "Oh," says the captain, "we have a peck of chaff that has got into this 5,000 bushels of wheat, and the only way to get rid of the chaff is to throw all the wheat overboard." Now, that is a great deal wiser than the talk of a great many Christians who want to throw overboard all the thousands and tens of thousands of souls who are the subjects of revivals. Throw all overboard because they are brought into the kingdom of God through great revivals, because there is a peck of chaff, a quart of chaff, a pint of chaff! I say, let them stay until the last day; the Lord will divide the chaff from the wheat. Do not be afraid of a great revival. Oh that such gales from heaven might sweep through all our churches! Oh, for such days as Richard Baxter saw in England, and Rodert McCheyne saw in Dundee! Oh, for such days as Johnathan Edwards saw in Northampton!

A GOOD STORY OF OLD JOHN LIVINGSTON.

I have often heard my father tell the fact that in the early part of this century a revival broke out at Somerville, N. J., and some people were very much agitated about it. They said: "Oh, you are going to bring too many people into the church at once," and they sent down to New Brunswick to get John Livingston to stop the revival. Well, there was no better soul in all the world than John Livingston. He went and looked at the revival; they wanted him to stop it. He stood in the pulpit on the Sabbath and looked over the solemn auditory, and he said: "This, brethern is in reality the work of God; beware how you try to stop it." And he was an old man, leaning heavily on his staff—a very old man. And he lifted that staff, and took hold of the small end of the staff, and began to let it fall slowly through between the finger and the thumb, and he said:

"Oh, thou impenitent, thou art falling now—falling from life, falling away from peace and heaven, falling as certainly, as that cane is falling through my hand—falling certainly, though perhaps falling slowly!" And the cane kept on falling through John Livingston's hand. The religious emotion in the audience was overpowering, and men saw a type of their doom, as the cane kept falling and falling, until the nob of the cane struck Mr. Livingston's hand, and he clasped it stoutly and said: "But the grace of God can stop you as I stopped that cane," and then there was a gladness all through the house at the fact of pardon, and peace, and salvation. "Well," said the people after the service: "I guess you had better send Livingston home; he is making the revival worse." Oh, for gales from heaven to sweep all the continents! The danger of the church of God is not in revivals.

JESUS IS BOTH GOD AND MAN.

Again, my subject impresses me with the fact that Jesus was God and man in the same being. Here he is in the back part of the boat. Oh, how tired he looks; what sad dreams he must have! Look at his countenance; he must be thinking of the cross to come. Look at him, he is a man—bone of our bone, flesh of our flesh. Tired, he falls asleep; he is a man. But then I find Christ at the prow of the boat; I hear him say: "Peace be still," and I see the storm kneeling at his feet and the tempests folding their wings in his presence; he is God.

If I have sorrow and trouble and want sympathy I go and kneel down at the back of the boat and say: "Oh, Christ, weary one of Gennesaret, sympathize with all my sorrows, man of Nazareth, man of the cross." A man, a man. But if I want to conquer my spiritual

JESUS HEALING THE BLIND.

foes, if I want to get the victory over sin, death, and hell, I come to the front of the boat, and I kneel down, and I say: "Oh, Lord Jesus Christ, thou who dost hush the tempest, hush all my grief, hush all my temptation hush all my sin." A man, a man; a God, a God.

CHRIST CAN HUSH THE TEMPEST.

I learn once more from this subject that Christ can hush a tempest.

It did seem as if everything must go to ruin. The disciples had given up the idea of managing the ship, the crew were entirely demoralized, yet Christ rises, and he puts his foot on the storm, and it crouches at his feet. Oh, yes! Christ can hush the tempest. You have had trouble. Perhaps it was the little child taken away from you—the sweetest child of the household, the one who asked the most curious questions, and stood around you with the greatest fondness, and the spade cut down through your bleeding heart. Perhaps it was an only son, and your heart has ever since been like a desolated castle, the owls of the night hooting among the fallen arches and the crumbling stairways. Perhaps it was an aged mother. You always went to her with your troubles. She was in your home to welcome your children into life, and when they died she was there to pity you; that old hand will do you no more kindness; that white lock of hair you put away in the casket or in the locket didn't look as it usually did when she brushed it away from her wrinkled brow in the home circle or in the country church. Or your property gone; you said: "I have so much bank stock, I have so many government securities, I have so many houses, I have so many farms—all gone, all gone." Why, sir, all the storms that ever trampled with their thunders, all the shipwrecks, have not been worse than

THE STORMY PASSAGE.

this to you. Yet you have not been completely overthrown. Why? Christ says: I have that little one in my keeping. I can care for him as well as you can, better than you can, O bereaved mother! Hushing the tempest. When your property went away, God said: "There are treasures in heaven, in banks that never break. Jesus hushing the tempest. There is one storm into which we will all have to run. The moment when we let go of this world and try to take hold of the next we will want all the grace possible. Yonder I see a Christian soul rocking on the surges of death; all the powers of darkness seem let out against that soul—the whirling wave, the thunder of the sky, the shriek of the wind, all seem to unite together; but that soul is not troubled there is no sighing, there are no tears; plenty of tears in the room at the departure, but he weeps no tears—calm, satisfied, and peaceful; all is well. By the flash of the storm you see the harbor just ahead, and you are making for that harbor. All shall be well, Jesus being our guide.

> "Into the harbor of heaven now we glide;
>   We're home at last, home at last.
> Softly we drift on the bright, silv'ry tide,
>   We're home at last.
>
> "Glory to God! all our dangers are o'er,
> We stand secure on the glorified shore;
> Glory to God! we will shout ever more,
> We'er home at last."

IN CANA, OF GALILEE.

A MARRIAGE FEAST.

[Delivered near Cana, of Galilee, December, 22, 1889.]

"*Thou hast kept the good wine until now.*" John ii, 10.

THE WEDDING IN CANA.

STANDING not far off from the demolished town of what was once called Cana of Galilee, I bethink myself of our Lord's first manhood miracle, which has been the astonishment of the ages. My visit last week to that place makes vivid in my mind that beautiful occurrence in Christ's ministry. My text brings us to a wedding in that village. It is a wedding in common life, two plain people having pledged each other, hand and heart, and their friends having come in for congratulation. The joy is not the less because there are no pretension. In each other they find all the future they want. The daisy in the cup on the table may mean as much as a score of artistic garlands fresh from the hot-house. When a daughter goes off from home with nothing but a plain father's blessing and a plain mother's love she is missed as much as though she were a princess. It seems hard, after the parents have sheltered her for eighteen years, that in a few short months her affections should have been carried off by another, but mother remembers how it was in her own case when she was young, and so she braces up until the wedding has passed, and the banqueters are gone, and she has a good cry all alone.

THE MIRACLE AT THE WEDDING.

Well, we are to-day at the wedding of Cana of Galilee. Jesus and his mother have been invited. It is evident that there are more people there than were expected. Either some people have come who were not invited, or more invitations have been sent out than it was supposed would be accepted. Of course there is not enough supply of wine. You know that there is nothing more embarrassing to a housekeeper than a scant supply. Jesus sees the embarrassment, and he comes up immediately to relieve it. He sees standing six water-pots. He orders the servants to fill them with water, then waves his hand over the water, and immediately it is wine—real wine. Taste of it, and see for yourselves; no logwood in it, no strychine in it, but first-rate wine. I will not now be diverted to the question so often discussed in my own country, whether it is right to drink wine. I am describing the scene as it was. When God makes wine he makes the very best wine, and 130 gallons of it standing around in these water-pots—wine so

A MARRIAGE FEAST.

good that the ruler of the feast tastes it and says: "Why, this is really better than anything we have had! Thou hast kept the good wine until now." Beautiful miracle! A prize was offered to the person who should write the best essay about the miracle in Cana. Long manuscripts were presented in the competition, but a poet won the prize by just this one line descriptive of the miracle:

"The unconscious water saw its God and blushed."

THE WONDERFUL SYMPATHY OF CHRIST.

We learn from this miracle, in the first place, that Christ has sympathy with housekeepers. You might have thought that Jesus would have said: "I can not be bothered with household deficiency of wine. It is not for me, lord of heaven, of earth, to become caterer to this feast. I have vaster things than this to attend to." Not so said Jesus. The wine gave out and Jesus, by miraculous power, came to the rescue. Does there ever come a scant supply in your household? Have you to make a very close calculation? Is it hard work for you to carry on things decently and respectably? If so, don't sit down and cry; don't go out and fret, but go to him who stood in the house in Cana of Galilee. Pray in the parlor! Pray in the kitchen! Let there be no room in your house unconsecrated by the voice of prayer. If you have a microscope put under it one drop of water and see the insects floating about, and when you see that God makes them, come to the conclusion that he will take care of you and feed you— Oh, ye of little faith!

A boy asked if he might sweep the snow from the steps of a house. The lady of the household said: "Yes; you seem very poor." He says: "I am very poor." She says: " Don't you sometimes get discouraged and feel that God is going to let you starve?" The lad looked up in the woman's face and said: "Do you think God will let me starve when I trust him and then do the best I can?" Enough theology for older people. Trust in God and do the best you can. Amidst all the worriments of housekeeping go to him; he will help you control your temper, and supervise your domestics, and entertain your guests, and manage your home economies. There are hundreds of women weak, and nervous, and exhausted with the cares of housekeeping. I commend you to the Lord Jesus Christ as the best adviser and the most efficient aid—the Lord Jesus who performed his first miracle to relieve a housekeeper.

THE ABUNDANCE OF CHRIST'S GIVING.

I learn also from this miracle that Christ does things in abundance. I think a small supply of wine would have made up for the deficiency. I think certainly they must have had enough for half of the guests. One gallon of this wine will do; certainly five gallons will be enough; certainly ten. But Jesus goes on, and he gives them 30 gallons, and 40 gallons, and 50 gallons, and 70 gallons, and 100 gallons, and 130 gallons of the very best wine.

It is just like him, doing everything on the largest and most generous scale. Does Christ, our creator, go forth to make leaves? He makes them by the whole forest full; notched like the fern, or silvered like the aspen, or broad like the palm; thickest in the tropics, Oregon forests.

Does he go forth to make flowers? He makes plenty of them; they flame from the hedge, they hang from the top of the grapevine in blossoms, they roll in the blue wave of the violets, they toss their white surf into the

spiræa—enough for every child's hand a flower, enough to make for every brow a chaplet, enough with beauty to cover up the ghastliness of all the graves.

Does he go forth to create water? He pours it out, not by the cup full, but by a river full, a lake full, an ocean full, pouring it out until all the earth has enough to drirk' and enough with which to wash.

Does Jesus, our Lord, provide redemption? It is not a little salvation for this one, a little for that, and a little for the other, but enough for all—"Whosoever will, let him come." Each man an ocean full for himself. Promises for the young, promises for the old, promises for the lowly, promises for the blind, for the halt, for the outcast. for the abandoned. Pardon for all, comfort for all, mercy for all, heaven for all; not merely a cupful of gospel glory, but 130 gallons. Ay, the tears of godly repentance are all gathered up into God's bottle, and some day, standing before the throne, we will lift our cup of delight and ask that it be filled with the wine of heaven, and Jesus, from that bottle of tears, will begin to pour in the cup, and we will cry: "Stop, Jesus, we do not want to drink our own tears!" and Jesus will say: "Know ye not that the tears of earth are the wine of heaven?" Sorrow may endure, but joy cometh in the morning.

TRY TO MAKE OTHERS HAPPY.

I remark further, Jesus does not shadow the joys of others with his own griefs. He might have sat down in that wedding and said: "I have so much trouble, so much poverty, so much persecution, and the cross is coming; I shall not rejoice, and the gloom of my face and of my sorrows shall be cast over all this group." So said not Jesus. He said to himself: "Here are two persons starting out in married life. Let it be a joyful occasion. I will hide my own griefs. I will kindle their joy." There are many not so wise as that. I know a household where there are many little children where for two years the musical instrument has been kept shut because there has been trouble in the house. Alas for the folly! Parents saying: "We will have no Christmas tree this coming holiday because there has been trouble in the house. Hush that laughing up.stairs! How can there be any joy when there has been so much trouble?" And so they make everything consistently doleful, and send their sons and daughters to ruin with the gloom they throw around them.

Oh, my dear friends, do you not know those children will have trouble enough of their own after awhile? Be glad they can not appreciate all yours. Keep back the cup of bitterness from your daughter's lips. When your head is down in the grass of the tomb poverty may come to her, betrayal to her, bereavement to her. Keep back the sorrows as long as you can. Do you not know that your son may, after awhile, have his heart broken? Stand between him and all harm. You may not fight his battles long; fight them while you may. Throw not the chill of your own despondency over his soul; rather be like Jesus, who came to the wedding hiding his own grief and kindling the joys of others. So I have seen the sun, on a dark day, struggling amidst the clouds, black, ragged, and portentious, but after awhile the sun, with golden spa heaved back the blackness, and the sun laughed to the lake, and the lake laughed to the sun, and from horizon to horizon, under the saffron sky, the water was all turned into wine.

CHRIST FAVORS THE LUXURIES OF LIFE.

I learn from this miracle that Christ is not impatient

with the luxuries of life. It was not necessary that they should have that wine. Hundreds of people have been married without any wine. We do not read that any of the other provisions fell short. When Christ made the wine it was not a necessity, but a positive luxury. I do not believe that he wants us to eat hard bread and sleep on hard mattresses, unless we like them the best. I think, if circumstances will allow, we have a right to the luxuries of dress, the luxuries of diet, and the luxuries of residence. There is no more religion in an old coat than in a new one. We can serve God drawn by golden-plated harness as certainly as when we go a-foot. Jesus Christ will dwell with us under a fine ceiling as well as under a thatched roof, and when you can get wine made out of water drink as much of it as you can.

What is the difference between a Chinese mud hovel and an American home? What is the difference between the rough bear-skins of the Russian boor and the outfit of an American gentleman? No difference except that which the gospel of Christ, directly or indirectly, has caused. When Christ shall have vanquished all the world I suppose every house will be a mansion, and every garment a robe, and every horse an arch-necked courser, and every carraige a glittering vehicle, and every man a king, and every woman a queen, and the whole earth a paradise; the glories of the natural world harmonizing with the glories of the material world until the very bells of the horses shall jingle the praises of the Lord.

CHRIST DOES NOT DENY US JOYS.

I learn further from this miracle that Christ has no impatience with festal joy, otherwise he would not have accepted the invitation to that wedding. He certainly would not have done that which increased the hilarity.

A MARRIAGE EEAST.

There may have been many in that room who were happy, but there was not one of them that did so much for the joy of the wedding party as Christ himself. He was the chief of the banqueters. When the wine gave out he supplied it, and so, I take it, he will not deny us the joys that are positively festal.

I think the children of God have more right to laugh than any other people and to clap their hands as loudly. There is not a single joy denied them that is given to any other people. Christianity does not clip the wings of the soul. Religion does not frost the flowers. What is Christianity? I take it to be simply a proclamation from the throne of God of emancipation for all the enslaved, and if man accepts the terms of that proclamation and becomes free has he not a right to be merry? Suppose a father has an elegant mansion and large grounds? To whom will he give the first privilege of these grounds? Will he say: "My children, you must not walk through these paths, or sit down under these trees, or pluck this fruit. These are for outsiders. They may walk in them." No father would say anything like that. He would say: "The first privileges in all the grounds and all of my house shall be for my own children." And yet men try to make us believe that God's children are on the limits, and the chief refreshments and enjoyments of life are for outsiders and not for his own children. It is stark atheism. There is no innocent beverage too rich for God's child to drink; there is no robe too costly for him to wear; there is no hilarity too great for him to indulge in, and no house too splendid for him to live in. He has a right to the joys of earth; he shall have a right to the joys of heaven. Though tribulation, and trial, and hardship may come unto him let him rejoice. "Rejoice in the Lord, ye

SITTING UNDER THE VINE.

righteous; and again I say, rejoice."

CHRIST WITH US IN OUR EXTREMITY—A STORY.

I remark again that Christ comes to us in the hour of our extremity. He knew the wine was giving out before there was any embarrassment or mortification. Why did he not perform the miracle sooner? Why wait until it was all gone and no help could come from any source and then come in and perform the miracle? This is Christ's way, and when he did come in at the hour of extremity he made first-rate wine, so that they cried out: "Thou hast kept the good wine until now." Jesus in the hour of extremity! He seems to prefer that hour.

In a Christian home in Poland great poverty had come, and on the week-day the man was obliged to move out of the house with his entire family. That night he knelt with his family and prayed to God. While they were kneeling in prayer there was a tap on the window-pane. They opened the window and there was a raven that the family had fed and trained, and in its bill a ring all set with precious stones, which was found out to be a ring belonging to the royal family. It was taken up to the king's residence and for the honesty of the man in bringing it back he had a house given to him, and a garden, and a farm. Who was it that sent the raven tapping on the window? The same God that sent the raven to feed Elijah by the brook of Cherith. Christ in the hour of extremity!

You mourned over your sins. You could not find the way out. You sat down and said: "God will not be merciful. He has cast me off;" but in that, the darkest hour of your history, light broke from the throne, and Jesus said "O wanderer, come home. I have seen all thy sorrows. In this, the hour of thy extremity, I offer thee pardon and everlasting life!"

Trouble came. You were almost torn to pieces by that trouble. You braced yourself up against it. You said: "I will be a stoic, and will not care;" but before you had got through making the resolution it broke down under you. You felt that all your resources were gone, and then Jesus came. "In the fourth watch of the night," the bible says, "Jesus came walking on the sea." Why did he not come in the first watch? or in the second watch? or in the third watch? I do not know. He came in the fourth, and gave deliverance to his disciples. Jesus in the last extremity!

I wonder if it will be so in our very last extremity. We shall fall suddenly sick, and doctors will come, but in vain. Something will say: "You must go." No one to hold us back, but the hands of eternity stretched out to pull us on. What then? Jesus will come to us, and as we say, "Lord Jesus, I am afraid of that water; I can not wade through to the other side," he will say, "Take hold of my arm;" and we will take hold of his arm, and then he will put his foot in the surf of the water, taking us down deeper, deeper, deeper, and our soul will cry: "All thy waves and billows have gone over me." They cover the feet, come to the knee, pass the girdle, and come to the head, and our soul cries out: "Lord Jesus Christ, I cannot hold thine arm any longer." Then Jesus will turn around, throw both his arms about us, and set us on the beach, far beyond the tossing of the billows. Jesus in the last extremity.

JESUS INVITES US TO A GRANDER WEDDING.

That wedding scene is gone now. The wedding-ring has been lost, the tankards have been broken, the house is down, but Jesus invites us to a grander wedding. You know that the bible says that the church is the lamb's wife, and the Lord will after awhile come to fetch her home, There will be gleaming of torches in the sky, and the trumpets of God will ravish the air with their music, and the church, robed in white, will put aside her veil, and look up into the face of her Lord the king, and the bridegroom will say to the bride: "Thou hast been faithful all these years! The mansion is ready! Home home! Thou art fair, my love!" And then he shall put upon her brow the crown of dominion, and table will be spread, and it will reach across the skies, and the mighty ones of heaven will come in, garlanded with beauty and striking their cymbals; and the bridegroom and the bride will stand at the head of the table, and the banqueters, looking up, will wonder and admire, and say: "That is Jesus the bridegroom. But the scar on his brow is covered with the coronet. and the stab in his side is covered with a robe!" and "That is the bride! The weariness of her earthly woe lost in the flush of this wedding triumph!"

There will be wine enough at that wedding; not coming up from the poisoned vats of earth, but the vineyards of God will press their ripest clusters, and the cups and the tankards will blush to the brim with the heavenly vintage, and then all the banqueters will drink standing. Esther, having come up from the bacchanalian revelry of Ahasuerus, where a thousand lords feasted, will be there. And the queen of Sheba, from the banquet of Solomon, will be there. And the mother of Jesus, from the wedding in Cana, will be there, And they all will agree that the earthly feasting was poor compared with that. Then, lifting their chalices in that holy light, they shall cry to the Lord of the feast: "Thou hast kept the good wine until now."

IN BEYROOT.

THE SKY ANTHEM.

[A Christmas Sermon delivered at Beyroot, Palestine, December, 24, 1889.]
"Glory to God in the highest, and on earth, peace, good will toward men." Luke, ii, 14.

CHRISTMAS EVE IN PALESTINE.

AT last I have what I longed for, a Christmas eve in the Holy land. This is the time of year that Christ landed. He was a December Christ. This is the chill air through which he descended. I look up through these Christmas skies, and I see no loosened star hastening southward to halt above Bethlehem, but all the stars suggest the star of Bethlehem.

No more need that any of them run along the sky to point downward. In quietude they kneel at the feet of him who, though once an exile, is now enthroned forever. Fresh up from Bethlehem I am full of the scenes suggested by a visit to that village. You know that whole region of Bethlehem is famous in bible story. There were the waving harvests of Boaz in which Ruth gleaned for herself and weeping Naomi. There David the warrior with thirty and three men of unheard of self-denial broke through the Philistine army to get him a drink. It was to that region that Joseph and Mary came to have their names enrolled in the census. That is what the scripture means when it says they came "to be taxed," for people did not in those days rush after the assessors of tax any more than they now do.

The village inn was crowded with the strangers who had come up by the command of government to have their names in the census, so that Joseph and Mary were obliged to lodge in the stables. You have seen some of those large stone buildings in the center of which the camels were kept, while running out from this center in all directions there were rooms, in one of which Jesus was born. Had his parents been more showily appareled, I have no doubt they would have found more comfortable entertainment. That night in the fields the shepherds, with crook and kindled fires, were watching their flocks, when hark to the sound of voices strangely sweet! Can it be that the maidens of Bethlehem have come out to serenade the weary shepherds? But now a light stoops upon them like the morning, so that the flocks arise, shaking their snowy fleece and bleating to their drowsy young. The heavens are filled with armies of light, and the earth quakes under the harmony as, echoed back from cloud to cloud.

it rings over the midnight hills: "Glory to God in the highest, and on earth peace, good will to men!" It seems the crown of royalty, and dominion, and power which Christ left behind him was hung on the sky in sight of Bethlehem. Who knows but that that crown may have been mistaken by the wise men for the star running and pointing downward.

INDIGENCE NOT DEGREDATION.

My subject, in the first place, impresses me with the fact that indigence is not always significant of degradation! When princes are born heralds announce it, and cannon thunder it, and flags wave it, and illuminations set cities on fire with the tidings. Some of us in England or America remember the time of rejoicing when the prince of Wales was born. You can remember the gladness throughout Christendom at the nativity in the palace at Madrid. But when our glorious prince was born there was no rejoicing on earth. Poor and growing poorer, yet the heavenly recognition that Christmas night shows the truth of the proposition that indigence is not always significant of degradation.

In all ages there have been great hearts throbbing under rags, tender sympathies under rough exterior, gold in the quartz, Parian marble in the quarry, and in every stable of privation wonders of excellence that have been the joy of the heavenly host. All the great deliverers of literature and of nations were born in homes without affluence, and from their own privation learned to speak and fight for the oppressed. Many a man has held up his pine-knot light from the wilderness until all nations and generations have seen it, and off of his hard crust of penury has broken the bread of knowledge and religion for the starving millions of the race. Poetry, and science, and literature, and commerce, and laws, and constitutions, and liberty, like Christ, were born in a manger. All the great thoughts which have decided the destiny of nations started in obscure corners, and had Herods who wanted to slay them, and Iscariots who betrayed them, and rabbles that crucified them, and sepulchers that confined them until they burst forth in glorious resurrection. Strong character, like the rhododendron, in an Alpine plant that grows faster in the storm. Men are like wheat, worth all the more for being flailed. Some of the most useful people would never have come to positions of usefulness had they not been ground and pounded and hammered in the foundry of disaster. When I see Moses coming up from the ark of bulrushes to be the greatest lawgiver of the ages, and Amos from tending the herds to make Israel tremble with his prophecies, and David from the sheepcot to sway the poet's pen and the king's scepter, and Peter from the fishing net to be the great preacher at the Pentecost, I find proof of the truth of my proposition that indigence is not always significant of degradation.

DUTY AND BLESSING.

My subject also impresses me with the thought that it is while at our useful occupations that we have the divine manifestations. Had those shepherds gone that night into Bethlehem and risked their flocks among the wolves they would not have heard the song of the angels. In other words, that man sees most of God and heaven who minds his own business. We all have our posts of duty, and standing there God appears to us. We are all shepherds or shepherdesses, and we have our flocks of cares, and annoyances, and anxieties, and we must tend them.

We sometimes hear very good people say: "If I had a month or a year or two to do nothing but attend to religious things I would be a great deal better than I am now." You are mistaken. Generally the best people are the busy people. Elisha was plowing in the field when the prophetic mantle fell upon him. Matthew was attending to his custom-house duties when Christ commanded him to follow. James and John were mending their nets when Christ called them to be fishers of men. Had they been snoring in the sun Christ would not have called their indolence into the apostleship. Gideon was at work with the flail on the thrashing floor when he saw the angel. Saul was with great fatigue hunting up the lost asses when he found the crown of Israel. The prodigal son would never have reformed and wanted to have returned to his father's house if he had not first gone into business; though it was swine-feeding. Not once out of a hundred times will a lazy man become a Christian. Those who have nothing to do are in very unfavorable circumstances for the receiving of divine manifestations. It is not when you are in idleness, but when you are, like the Bethlehem shepherds. watching your flocks, that the glory descends and there is joy among the angels of God over your soul penitent and forgiven.

RELIGION IS JOYFUL.

My subject also strikes at the delusion that the religion of Christ is dolorous and grief-infusing. The music that broke through the midnight heavens was not a dirge, but an anthem. It shook joy over the hills. It not only dropped upon the shepherds but it sprang upward among the thrones. The robe of a Saviour's righteousness is not black. The Christian life is not made up of weeping and cross-bearing and war-waging. Through the revelation of that Christmas night I find that religion is not a groan but a song. In a world of sin and sick-bed and sepulchers we must have trouble, but in the darkest night the heavens part with angelic song. You may, like Paul, be shipwrecked, but I exhort you to be of good cheer, for you shall all escape safe to the land. Religion does not show itself in the elongation of the face and the cut of the garb. The Pharisee who puts his religion into his phylactery has none left for his heart. Fretfulness and complaining do not belong to the family of Christian graces which move into the heart when the devil moves out. Christianity does not frown upon amusements and recreations. It is not a cynic, it is not a shrew, it chokes no laughter, it quenches no light, it defaces no art. Among the happy it is the happiest. It is just as much at home on the play ground as it is in the church. It is just as graceful in the charade as it is in the psalm-book. It sings just as well in Surrey gardens as it prays in St. Paul's. Christ died that we might live. Christ walked that we might ride. Christ wept that we might laugh.

THE MANGER AND THRONE.

Again, my subject impresses me with the fact that glorious endings sometimes have very humble beginnings. The straw pallet was the starting point, but the shout in the midnight sky revealed what would be the glorious consummation. Christ on Mary's lap, Christ on the throne of universal dominion—what an humble starting! What a glorious ending! Grace begins on a small scale in the heart. You see only men as trees walking. The grace of God in the heart is a feeble spark, and Christ has to keep both hands over it lest it be blown out. What an humble beginning! But look at the same man when he has entered heaven. No crown able to express his royalty. No palace able to express his wealth. No scepter able to express his power and his dominion. Drinking from the fountain that drips from the everlasting rock. Among the harpers harping with their harps. On a sea of glass mingled with fire. Before the throne of God, to go no more out forever. The spark of grace that Christ had to keep both hands over lest it come to extinction, having flamed up into honor, glory and immortality. What humble starting! What glorious consummation!

The new testament church was on a small scale. Fishermen watched it. Against the uprising walls crashed infernal enginery. The world said anathema. Ten thousand people rejoiced at every seeming defeat and said: "Aha! aha! so we would have it." Martyrs on fire cried: "How long, O Lord, how long?" Very humble starting, but see the difference at the consummation, when Christ with his almighty arm has struck off the last chain of human bondage, and Himalayas shall be Mount Zion, and Pyrenees Moriah, and oceans the walking place of him who trod the wave cliffs of stormed Tiberias, and island shall call to island, sea to sea, continent to continent, and the song of the world's redemption rising, the heavens, like a great sounding board, shall strike back the shout of salvation to the earth until it rebounds again to the throne of God, and all heaven, rising on their thrones beat time with their scepters. Oh, what an humble beginning! What a glorious ending! Throne linked to a manger, heavenly mansions to a stable.

THE DOUBLE MISSION OF CHRIST.

My subject also impresses me with the effect of Christ's mission upward and downward. Glory to God, peace to man. When God sent his son into the world angels discovered something new in God, something they had never seen before. Not power, not wisdom, not love. They knew all that before. But when God sent his son into this world then the angels saw the spirit of self-denial in God, the spirit of self-sacrifice in God. It is easier to love an angel on his throne than a thief on the cross, a seraph in his worship than an adultress in her crime. When the angels saw God—the God who would not allow the most insignificant angel in heaven to be hurt—give up his son, his only son, they saw something that they had never thought of before, and I do not wonder that when Christ started out on that pilgrimage the angels in heaven clapped their wings in triumph and called on all the hosts of heaven to help them celebrate it, and sang so loud that the Bethlehem shepherds heard it: "Glory to God in the highest."

But it was also to be a mission of peace to man. Infinite holiness—accumulated depravity. How could they ever come together? The gospel bridges over the distance. It brings God to us. It takes us to God. God in us, and we in God. Atonement! Atonement! Justice satisfied, sin forgiven, eternal life secured, heaven built on a manger.

But it was to be the pacification of all individual and international animosities. What a sound this word of peace had in the Roman Empire that boasted of the number of people it had massacred, that prided itself on the number of the slain, that rejoiced at the trembling providences. Sicily, and Sardinia, and Macedonia, and Egypt had bowed to her sword and crouched at the cry of her war eagles. She gave her chief honor to Scipio, and Fabius, and Cæsar—all men of blood. What contempt they must have had there for the penniless, unarmed Christ in the garb of a Nazarene, starting out to conquer all nations. There never was a place on earth where that word peace sounded so offensively to the ears of the multitudes as in the Roman empire. They did not want peace. The greatest music they ever heard was the clanking chains of their captives. If all the blood that has been shed in battle could be gathered together it would bear up a navy. The club that struck Abel to the earth has its echo in the butcheries of all ages. Edmund Burke, who gave no wild statistics, said that there had been spent in slaughter $35,-000,000,000 or what would be equal to that, but he had not seen into our times, when in our own day, in America, we expended $3,000,000,000 in civil war.

THE VISION OF BATTLES.

Oh, if we could now take our position on some high point and see the world's armies march past! There go the hosts of Israel through a score of Red seas—one of water, the rest of blood. There go Cyrus and his army, with infuriate yell rejoicing over the fall of the gates of

WAR IN ANCIENT TIMES.

Babylon. There goes Alexandei, leading forth his hosts, and conquering all the world but himself, the earth reeling with the battle gash of Arbela and Persepolis. There goes Ferdinand Cortes, leaving his butchered enemies on the table-lands, once fragrant with vanilla and covered over with groves of flowering cacao. There goes the great Frenchman, leading his army down through Egypt like one of its plagues and up through Russia like one of its own icy blasts. Yonder is the grave trench under the shadow of Sebastopol. There are the ruins of Delhi and Allahabad, and yonder are the inhuman Sepoys and the brave regiments under Havelock avenging the insulted flag of Britain, while cut right through the heart of my native land is a trench in which there lie 1,000,000 northern and southern dead.

Oh, the tears! Oh, the blood! Oh, the long marches! Oh, the hospital wounds! Oh, the martyrdom! Oh, the death! But brighter than the light which flashed on all these swords and shields and musketry is the light that fell on Bethlehem, and louder than the bray of the trumpets, and the neighing of the charges, and the crash of the walls, and the groaning of the dying armies, is the song that unrolls this moment from the sky, sweet as though all the bells of heaven rung a jubilee, "Peace on earth, good will toward men." Oh, when will the day come—God hasten it! —when the swords shall be turned into plowshares, and the fortresses shall be remodeled into churches, and the men of blood battling for renown shall become good soldiers for Jesus Christ, and the cannon now striking down whole columns of death shall thunder the victories of the truth.

When we think of the whole world saved we are apt to think of the few people that now inhabit it. Only a very few compared with the population to come. And what a small part cultivated. Do you know it has been authentically estimated that three-fourths of Europe is yet all barrenness, and that nine hundred and ninety-nine one-thousandth part of the entire globe is uncultivated? This is all to be cultivated, all inhabited, and all gospelized. Oh, what tears of repentance when nations begin to weep! Oh, what supplications when continents begin to pray! Oh, what rejoicing when hemispheres begin to sing! Churches will worship on the places where this very hour smokes the blood of human sacrifice, and wandering through the snake-infested jungles of Africa Christ's heel will bruise the serpent's head. Oh, when the trumpet of salvation shall be sounded everywhere and the nations are redeemed, a light will fall upon every town brighter than that which fell upon Bethlehem, and more overwhelming than the song that fell on the pasture fields where the flocks fed there will be a song louder than the voice of the storm-lifted oceans, "Glory to God in the higest," and from all nations, and kindred, and people, and tongues will come the response: "And on earth peace, and good will toward men!"

A TOUCHING STORY.

On this Christmas we bring you good tidings of great joy. Pardon for all sin, comfort for all trouble, and life for the dead. Shall we now take this Christ into our hearts? The time is passing. This is the closing of the year. How the time speeds by. Put your hand on your heart—one, two, three. Three times less it will beat. Life is passing like gazelles over the plain. Sorrows hover like petrels over the sea. Death swoops like a vulture from the mountains. Misery rolls up to our ears like waves. Heavenly songs fall to us like stars.

THE SKY ANTHEM.   135

I wish you a merry Christmas, not with worldly dispensations, but merry with gospel gladness, merry with pardoned sin, merry with hope of reunion in the skies with all your loved ones who have preceded you. In that grandest and best sense a merry Christmas.

And God grant that in our final moment we may have as bright a vision as did the dying girl when she said: "Mother"—pointing with her thin, white hand through the window—"Mother, what is that beautiful land out yonder beyond the mountains, the high mountains?" "Oh," said the mother, "my darling, there are no mountains within sight of our home." "Oh, yes,', she said, "Don't you see them—that beautiful land beyond the mountains out there, just beyond the high mountains?"

The mother looked down into the face of her dying child and said: "My dear I think that must be heaven that you see." "Well, then," she said, "father, you come, and with your strong arms carry me over those mountains into that beautiful land beyond the high mountains." "No," said the weeping father, "my darling, I can't go with you." "Well," she said, clapping her hands, "never mind; never mind; I see yonder a shining one coming. He is coming now, in his strong arms to carry me over the mountains to the beautiful land—over the mountains, over the high mountains."

BETHLEHEM.

IN VIENNA.

THE HALF NOT TOLD.
[Delivered in Vienna, January, 5th., 1890.]
"*Behold, the half was not told me.*" *I Kings x.,* 7.

THE TWO CIRCLES.

APPEARING before you to-day, my mind yet agitated with the scenery of the Holy land, from which we have just arrived, you will expect me to revert to some of the scenes once enacted there. Mark a circle around Lake Galilee, and another circle around Jerusalem, and you describe the two regions in which cluster memories of more events than in any other two circles. Jerusalem was a spell of fascination that will hold me the rest of my life. Solomon had resolved that that city should be the center of all sacred, regal, and commercial magnificence. He set himself to work, and monopolized the surrounding desert as a highway for his caravans. He built the city of Palmyra around one of the principal wells of the east, so that all the long trains of merchandise from the east were obliged to stop there, pay toll, and leave part of their wealth in the hands of Solomon's merchants. He manned the fortress Thapsacus at the chief ford of the Euphrates and put under guard everything that passed there. The three great products of Palestine—wine pressed from the richest clusters and celebrated all the world over; oil, which in that hot country is the entire substitute for butter and lard, and was pressed from the olive branches until every tree in the country became an oil-well, and honey, which was the entire substitute for sugar—these three great products of the country Solomon exported and received in return fruits, and precious woods, and the animals of every clime.

He went down to Ezion-geber and ordered a fleet of ships to be constructed, oversaw the workmen, and watched the launching of the flotilla which was to go out on more than a year's voyage to bring home the wealth of the then known world. He heard that the Egyptian horses were large and swift and long-maned and round-limbed, and he resolved to purchase them, giving $85 apiece for them, putting the best of these horses in his own stall, and selling the surplus to foreign potentates at great profit.

He heard that there was the best of timber on Mount Lebanon and he sent out 180,000 men to hew down the forest and drag the timber through the mountain gorges, to construct it into rafts to be floated to Joppa and from thence to be drawn by ox-teams twenty-five miles across the land to Jerusalem. He heard that there were beautiful flowers in other lands. He sent for them, planted them in his own garden, and to this very day there are flowers found in the ruins of that city such as are to be found in no other part of Palestine, the lineal descendants of the very flowers that Solomon planted. He heard that in foreign groves there were birds of richest voice and most luxuriant wing. He sent out people to catch them and bring them there, and he put them into cages.

Stand back now and see this long train of camels coming up to the king's gate, and the ox-trains from

Egypt, gold and silver and precious stones, and beasts of every hoof, and birds of every wing, and fish of every scale! See the peacocks strut under the cedars, and the horsemen run, and the chariots wheel! Hark to the orchestra! Gaze upon the dance! Not stopping to look into the wonders of the temple step right on to the causeway, and pass up to Solomon's palace.

A VISION OF BEAUTY.

Here we find ourselves amid a collection of buildings on which the king had lavished the wealth of many empires. The genius of Hiram, the architect, and of the other artists is here seen in the long line of corridors, and the suspended gallery, and the approach to the throne; Traceried window opposite traceried window. Bronzed ornaments bursting into lotus, and lily, and pomegranate. Chapiters surrounded by network of leaves in which imitation fruit seemed suspended as in hanging baskets. Three branches—so Josephus tells us—three branches sculptured on the marble, so thin and subtle that even the leaves seemed to quiver. A laver capable of holding 500 barrels of water on 600 brazen ox heads, which gushed with water and filled the whole place with coolness and crystalline brightness and musical splash. Ten tables chased with chariot wheel, and lion, and cherubim. Solomon sat on a throne of ivory. At the seating place of the throne, on each end of the steps, a brazen lion. Why, my friends, in that place they trimmed their candles with snuffers of gold, and they cut their fruits with knives of gold, and they washed their faces in basins of gold, and they scooped out the ashes with shovels of gold, and they stirred the altar fires with tongs of gold. Gold reflected in the water! Gold flashed from the apparel! Gold blazing in the crown! Gold, gold, gold!

Of course the news of the affluence of that place went out everywhere by every caravan and by wing of every ship, until soon the streets of Jerusalem are crowded with curiosity-seekers. What is that long procession approaching Jerusalem? I think from the pomp of it there must be royalty in the train. I smell the breath of the spices which are brought as presents, and I hear the shout of the drivers, and I see the dust-covered caravan, showing that they come from far away. Cry the news up to the palace. The queen of Sheba advances. Let all the people come out to see. Let the mighty men of the land come out on the palace corridors. Let Solomon come down the stairs of the palace before the queen has alighted. Shake out the cinnamon and the saffron, and the calamus, and the frankincense, and pass it into the treasure house. Take up the diamonds until they glitter in the sun.

THE QUEEN OF SHEBA.

The queen of Sheba alights. She enters the palace. She washes at the bath. She sits down at the banquet. The cup-bearers bow. The meat smokes. The music trembles in the dash of the waters from the modern sea. Then she rises from the banquet, and walks through the conservatories, and gazes on the architectures, and she asks Solomon many strange questions, and then she learns about the religion of the Hebrews, and she then and there becomes a servant of the Lord God.

She is overwhelmed. She begins to think that all the spices she brought, and all the precious wood which are intended to be turned into harps and psaltreies and into railings for the causeway between the temple and the palace, and the $1,800,000 in money—she begins to think that all these presents amount to nothing in such a place, and she is almost ashamed that she has brought them, and she says within herself: "I heard a great deal about this place, and about this wonderful religion of the Hebrews, but I find it far beyond my highest anticipations. I must add more than fifty per cent to what has been related. It exceeds everything that I could have expected. The half, the half was not told me:"

WOMEN, WEALTH, RELIGION.

I learn from this subject what a beautiful thing it is when social position and wealth surrender themselves to God. When religion comes to a neighborhood the first to receive it are the women. Some men say it is because they are weak minded. I say it is because they have quicker preception of what is right, more ardent affection, and capacity for sublimer emotion. After the women have received the gospel then all the distressed and the poor of both sexes, those who have no friends, except Jesus. Last of all come the greatly prospered. Alas, that it is so!

If there are those who have been favored of fortune, or, as I might better put it, favored of God, surrender all you have and all you expect to be to the Lord who blessed this queen of Sheba. Certainly you are not ashamed to be found in this queen's company. I am glad that Christ has had his imperial friends in all ages —Elizabeth Christina, queen of Prussia; Maria Feodorovna, queen of Russia; Maria, empress of France; Helena, the imperial mother of Constantine; Arcadia, from her great fortunes building public baths in Constantinople and toiling for the alleviation of the masses; Queen Clotilda, leading her husband and 3,000 of his armed warriors to Christian baptism; Elizabeth of Burgundy, giving her jeweled glove to a beggar, and scattering great fortunes among the distressed; Prince Albert, singing "Rock of ages" in Windsor castle, and

Queen Victoria, incognita, reading the scriptures to a dying pauper.

I bless God that the day is coming when royalty will bring all its thrones, and music all its harmonies, and painting all its pictures, and sculpture all its statuary, and architecture all its pillars, and conquest all its scepters, and the queens of the earth, in long line advance, frankincense filling the air, and the camels laden with gold, shall approach Jerusalem, and the gates shall be hoisted, and the great burden of splendor shall be lifted into the palace of this greater than Solomon.

EARNESTNESS IN SEARCH OF TRUTH.

Again, my subject teaches me what is earnestness in the search of truth. Do you know where Sheba was? It was in Abyssinia, or some say in the southern part of Arabia Felix. In either case it was a great way off from Jerusalem. To get from there to Jerusalem she had to cross a country infested with bandits and go across blistering deserts. Why did not the queen of Sheba stay at home and send a committee to inquire about this new religion, and have the delegates report in regard to that religion and wealth of King Solomon? She wanted to see for herself and hear for herself. She could not do this by work of committee. She felt that she had a soul worth ten thousand kingdoms like Sheba and she wanted a robe richer than any woven by oriental shuttles, and she wanted a crown set with the jewels of eternity. Bring out the camels. Put on the spices! Gather up the jewels of the throne and put them on the caravan. Start now; no time to be lost. Goad on the camels. When I see that caravan, dust-covered, weary and exhausted, trudging on across the desert and among the bandits until it reaches Jerusalem, I say: "There is an earnest seeker after truth."

EARNEST SEEKERS.

But there are a great many who do not act in that way. They all want to get the truth, but they want the truth to come to them; they do not want to go to it. There are people who fold their arms and say: "I am ready to become a Christian at any time; if I am to be saved I shall be saved, and if I am to be lost I shall be lost." But Jerusalem will never come to you; you must go to Jerusalem. The religion of the Lord Jesus Christ will not come to you; you must go and get religion. Bring out the camels; put on all the sweet spices, all the treasures of the heart's affection. Start for the throne. Go in and hear the waters of salvation dashing in fountains all around about the throne. Sit down at the banquet—the wine pressed from the grapes of the heavenly Eshcol, the angels of God the cup-bearers. Goad on the camels. The bible declares it: "The queen of the south"—that is, this very woman I am speaking of—"the queen of the south shall rise up in judgment against this generation and condemn it; for she came from the uttermost parts of the earth to hear the wisdom of Solomon; and behold! a greater than Solomon is here." What infatuation, the sitting down in idleness expecting to be saved. "Strive to enter in at the straight gate. Ask, and it shall be given you; seek, and ye shall find; knock, and it shall be opened to you." Take the kingdom of heaven by violence. Urge on the camels!

RELIGION A SURPRISE.

Again, my subject impresses me with the fact that religion is a surprise to any one that gets it. This story of the new religion in Jerusalem and of the glory of King Solomon, who was a type of Christ—that story rolled on and on and was told by every traveler coming back from Jerusalem. The news goes on the wing of every ship and with every caravan, and you know a story enlarges as it is retold, and by the time that story gets down into the southern part of Arabia Felix and the queen of Sheba hears it, it must be a tremendous story. And yet this queen declares in regard to it, although she had heard so much and had her anticipations raised so high, the half, the half was not told her.

So religion is always a surprise to any one that gets it. The story of grace—an old story. Apostles preached it with rattle of chain; martyrs declared it with arm fire; deathbeds have affirmed it with visions of glory, and ministers of religion have sounded it through the lanes and the highways, and the chapels and the cathedrals. It has been cut into stone with chisel, and spread on the canvas with pencil; and it has been recited in the doxology of great congregations. And yet, when a man first comes to loook on the palace of God's mercy, and to see the royalty of Christ, and the wealth of this banquet, and the luxuries of his attendants, and the loveliness of his face, and the joy of his service, he exclaims with prayers, with tears, with sighs, with triumph: "The half—the half was not told me!"

I appeal to those who are Christians. Compare the idea you had of the joy of the Christian life before you become a Christian with the appreciation of that joy you have now since you have become a Christian, and you are willing to attest before angels and men that you never, in the days of your spiritual bondage, had any appreciation of what was to come. You are ready today to answer and say in regard to the discoveries you have made the mercy, and the grace, and the goodness of God: "The half—the half was not told me!"

Well, we hear a great deal about the good time that is coming to this world when it is to be girded with salvation. Holiness on the bells of the horses. The lion's mane patted by the hand of a babe. Ships of Tarshish bringing cargoes for Jesus, and the hard, dry, barren, winter-bleached, storm-scarred, thunder-split rock breaking into floods of bright water. Deserts into which dromedaries thrust their nostrils, because they were afraid of the simoon—deserts blooming into carnation roses and silver-tipped lillies.

It is an old story. Everybody tells it. Isaiah told it, John told it, Paul told it, Ezekiel told it, Luther told it, Calvin told it, John Milton told it—every-body tells it, and yet—and yet when the midnight shall fly the hills, and Christ shall marshall his great army, and China, dashing her idols into the dust, shall hear the voice of God and wheel into line, and India, destroying her Juggernant and snatching up her little children from the Ganges, shall hear the voice of God and wheel into line, and vine-covered Italy, and wheat-crowned Russia, and all the nations of the earth shall hear the voice of God and fall into line; then the church, which has been toiling and struggling through the centuries, robed and garlanded like a bride adorned for her husband, shall put aside her veil and look up into the face of the lord and king and say: The half—the half was not told me.

THE FINAL WONDER!

Well, there is coming a greater surprise to every Christian—a greater surprise than anything I have depicted. Heaven is an old story. Everybody talks about it. There is hardly a hymn in the hymn-book that does not refer to it. Children read about it in their Sabbath-school books. Aged men put on their spectacles to study it. We say it is a harbor from the storm. We call it home. We say it is the house of many mansions. We weave together all sweet, beautiful, delicate, exhilarant words; we weave them into letters, and then we spell it out in rose and lily and amaranth. And yet that place is going to be a surprise to the most intelligent Christian. Like the queen of Sheba the report has come to us from the far country, and many of us have started. It is a desert march, but we urge on the camels. What though our feet be blistered on the way? We are hastening to the palace. We take all our loves and hopes and Christian ambitions, as frankincense and myrrh and cassia to the great king. We must not rest. We must not halt. The night is coming on and it is not safe out here in the desert. Urge on the camels. I see the domes against the sky, and the houses of Lebanon, and the temples, and the gardens. See the fountains dancing in the sun, and the gates flash as they open to let in the poor pilgrim.

Send the word up to the palace that we are coming and that we are weary of the march of the desert. The king will come out and say: "Welcome to the palace; bathe in these waters; recline on these banks. Take this cinnamon, and frankincense, and myrrh, and put it upon a censer and swing it before the altar."

And yet, my friends, when heaven bursts upon us it will be a greater surprise than that—Jesus on the throne and we made like him! All our Christian friends surrounding us in glory! All our sorrows, and tears, and sins gone by forever! The thousands of thousands, the one hundred and forty and four thousand, the great multitudes that no man can number, will cry, world without end: "The half—the half was not told me!"

NAPOLEON WITNESSING THE BURNING OF MOSCOW.

IN PARIS.

DOWNFALL OF ATHALIAH.

[Delivered in Paris, Jan., 12th, 1890.]

"*Jehosheba, the daughter of King Joram, sister of Ahaziah, took Joash, the son of Ahaziah, and stole him from among the king's sons which were slain; and they hid him, even him and his nurse, in the bed-chamber from Athaliah, so that he was not slain. And he was with her hid in the house of the Lord six years,*" II *Kings*, xi., 2, 3.

A WORD TO GRANDMOTHERS.

GRANDMOTHERS are more lenient with their children's children than they were with their own. At 40 years of age, if discipline be necessary, chastisement is used, but at 70, the grandmother, looking upon the misbehavior of the grandchild, is apologetic and disposed to substitute confectionery for whip. There is nothing more beautiful than this mellowing of old age toward childhood. Grandmother takes out her pocket handkerchief and wipes her spetacles and puts them on, and looks down into the face of her mischievous and rebellious descendant, and says: "I don't think he meant to do it; let him off this time; I'll be responsible for his behavior in the future." My mother, with the second generation around her—a boisterous crew—said one day: "I suppose they ought to be disciplined, but I can't do it. Grandmothers are not fit to bring up grandchildren." But here, in my text, we have a grandmother of a different hue.

I have within a few days been at Jerusalem, where the occurrence of the text took place, and the whole scene came vividly before me while I was going over the site of the ancient temple and climbing the towers of the king's palace. Here in the text it is old Athaliah the queenly murderess. She ought to have been honorable. Her father was a king. Her husband was a king. Her son was a king. And yet we find her plotting for the extermination of the entire royal family, including her own grandchildren. The executioner's knives are sharpened. The palace is red with the blood of princes and princesses. On all sides are shrieks, and hands thrown up, and struggle, and death-groan. No mercy! Kill! Kill!

A WIFE STEALS A CHILD.

But while the ivory floors of the palace run with carnage, and the whole land is under the shadow of a great horror, a fleet-footed woman, a clergyman's wife, Jehosheba by name, stealthily approaches the imperial nursery, seizes upon the grandchild that had somehow

DOWNFALL OF ATHALIAH. 151

as yet escaped massacre, wraps it up tenderly but in haste, snuggles it against her, flies down the palace stairs, her heart in her throat lest she be discovered in this Christian abduction. Get her out of the way as quick as you can, for she carries a precious burden, even a young king. With this youthful prize she presses into the room of the ancient temple, the church of olden time, unwraps the young king and puts him down, sound asleep as he is, and unconscious of the peril that has been threatened; and there for six years he is secreted in that church apartment. Meanwhile old Athaliah smacks her lips with satisfaction and thinks that all the royal family are dead.

But the six years expire, and it is now time for young Joash to come forth and take the throne, and to push back into disgrace and death old Athaliah. The arrangements are all made for political revolution. The military come and take possession of the temple, swear loyalty to the boy Joash, and stand around for his defense. See the sharpened swords and burnished shields! Everything is ready. Now Joash, half affrighted at the armed tramp of his defenders, scared at the vociferation of his admirers, is brought forth in full regalia. The scroll of authority is put in his hands, the the coronet of government is put on his brow, and the people clapped, and waved, and huzzaed, and trumpeted. "What is that?" said Athaliah. "What is that sound over in the temple?" And she flies to see, and on her way they meet her and say: "Why, haven't you heard? You thought you had slain all the royal family, but Joash has come to light." Then the queenly murderess, frantic with rage, grabbed her mantle and tore it to tatters, and cried until she foamed at the mouth: "You have no right to crown my grandson. You have no right to take the government from my shoulders. Treason! Treason!" While she stood there crying that, the military started for her arrest, and she took a short cut through a back door of the temple and ran through the royal stables; but the battle-axes of the military fell on her in the barn-yard, and for many a day when the horses were being unloosed from the chariot after drawing out young Joash the fiery steeds would snort and rear passing the place, as they smelt the place of the carnage.

RIGHTEOUSNESS CANNOT BE EXTERMINATED.

The first thought I hand you from this subject is that the extermination of righteousness is an impossibility. When a woman is good, she is apt to be very good, and when she is bad she is apt to be very bad, and this Athaliah was one of the latter sort. She would exterminate the last scion of the house of David, through whom Jesus was to come. There was plenty of work for embalmers and undertakers. She would clear the land of all God-fearing and God-loving people. She would put an end to everything that could in anywise interfere with her imperial criminality. She folds her hands and says: "The work is done; it is completely done." Is it? In the swaddling clothes of that church apartment are wrapped the cause of God, in the cause of good government. That is the scion of the house of David; it is Joash, the Christian reformer; it is Joash, the friend of God; it is Joash, the demolisher of Baalitish idolatry. Rock him tenderly; nurse him gently. Athaliah, you may kill all the other children, but you cannot kill him. Eternal defences are thrown all around him, and this clergyman's wife, Johosheba, will snatch him up from the palace nursery, and will run up and down with him into the house of the Lord, and there

PAUL BEFORE THE COUNCIL.

she will hide him for six years, and at the end of that time he will come forth for your dethronement and obliteration.

PERSECUTIONS ARE FUTILE.

Well, my friends, just as poor a botch does the world always make of extinguishing righteousness. Superstition rises up and says: "I will just put an end to pure religion." Domitian slew 40,000 Christians. Diocletian slew 844,000 Christians. And the scythe of persecution has been swung through all ages, and the flames hissed, and the guillotine chopped, and the bastile groaned; but did the foes of Christianity exterminate it? Did they exterminate Alban, the first sacrifice; or Zuinglius, the Swiss reformer; or John Oldcastle, the Christian nobleman; or Abdallah, the Arabian martyr; or Anne Askew, or Sanders, or Cranmer? Great work of extermination they made of it. Just at the time when they thought they had slain all the royal family of Jesus some Joash would spring up and out and take the throne of power and wield a very scepter of Christian dominion.

INFIDELITY FAILS TO ANNIHILATE.

Infidelity says: "I'll just exterminate the bible," and the scriptures were thrown into the street for the mob to trample on, and they were piled up in the public squares and set on fire, and mountains of indignant contempt were hurled on them, and learned universities decreed the bible out of existence. Thomas Paine said: "In my 'Age of Reason' I have annihilated the scriptures. Your Washington is a pusillanimous Christian, but I am the foe of bibles and of churches." Oh, how many assaults upon that word! All the hostilities that have ever been created on earth are not to be compared with the hostilities against that one book. Said one man in his infidel desperation to his wife: "You must not be reading that bible," and he snatched it away from her. And though in that bible was a lock of hair of the dead child—the only child that God had ever given them—he pitched the book with its contents into the fire; and stirred it with the tongs and spat on it, and cursed it. and said: "Susan, never have any more of that damnable stuff here!"

How many individual and organized attempts have been made to exterminate that bible! Have they done it? Have they exterminated the British and Foreign Bible society? Have they exterminated the thousands of Christian institutions, whose only object is to multiply copies of the scriptures and throw them broadcast around the world? They have exterminated until instead of one or two copies of the bible in our homes we have eight or ten, and we pile them up in the corners for our Sabbath-school rooms and send great boxes of them everywhere.

If they get on as well as they are now going on in the work of extermination I do not know but that our children may live to see the millennium! Yea, if there should come a time of persecution in which all the known bibles of the earth should be destroyed, all these lamps of light that blaze in our pulpits and in our families extinguished. In the very day that infidelity and sin should be holding a jubilee over the universal extinction there would be in some closet of a backwoods church a secreted copy of the bible, and this Joash of eternal literature would come out and come up and take the throne, and the Athaliah of infidelity and persecution would fly out the back door of the palace and drop her miserable carcass under the hoofs of the horses of the king's stable. You can not exterminate Christianity! You cannot kill Joash!

THE OPPORTUNITIES FOR SAVING.

The second thought I hand you from my subject is, that there are oportunities in which we may save royal life. You know that profane history is replete with stories of strangled monarchs and of young princes who have been put out of the way. Here is the story of a young king saved. How Jehosheba. the clergyman's wife, must have trembled as she rushed into the imperial nursery and snatched up Joash. How she hushed him, lest by his cry he hinder the escape. Fly with him! Jehosheba, you hold in your arms the cause of God and good government. Fail, and he is slain. Succeed, and you turn the tide of the world's history in the right direction. It seems as if between that young king and his assassins there is nothing but the frail arm of a woman. But why should we spend our time in praising the bravery of expedition when God asks the same thing of you and me? All around us are the imperiled children of a great king.

They are born of almighty parentage and will come to a throne or a crown if permitted. But sin, the old Athaliah, goes forth to the massacre. Murderous temptations are out for the assassination. Valens, the emperor, was told that there was somebody in his realm who would usurp the throne and that the name of the man who should be the usurper would begin with the letters T. H. E. O. D., and the edict went forth from the emperor's throne: "Kill everybody whose name begins with T. H. E. O. D." And hundreds and thousands were slain, hoping by that massacre to put an end to that one usurper. But sin is more terrific in its denunciation. If matters not how you spell your

Love of Children   [*Pompeii Painting.*]

name, you come under its knife, under its sword, under its doom, unless there be some omnipotent relief brought to the rescue. But, blessed be God, there is such a thing as delivering a royal soul. Who will snatch away Joash?

PERSONS IN YOUR SUNDAY SCHOOL CLASS!

This afternoon, in your Sabbath-school class, there will be a prince of God—some one who may yet reign as king forever before the throne; there will be some one in your class who has a corrupt physical inheritance; there will be some one in your class who has a father and mother who do not know how to pray; there will be some one in your class who is destined to command in church or state—some Cromwell to dissolve a parliament, some Beethoven to touch the world's harp-strings, some John Howard to pour fresh air into the lazaretto, some Florence Nightengale to bandage the battle wounds, some Miss Dix to soothe the crazed brain, some John Frederick Oberlin to educate the besotted, some David Brainard to change the Indian's war-whoop to a Sabbath song, some John Wesley to marshall threefourths of Christendom, some John Knox to make queens turn pale, some Joash to demolish idolatry and strike for the kingdom of heaven.

There are sleeping in your cradles by night, there are playing in your nurseries by day, imperial souls waiting for dominion, and whichever side the cradle they get out will decide the destiny of empires. For each one of those children sin and holiness counted—Athaliah on one side and Jehosheba on the other. But I hear people say; "What's the use of bothering children with religious instruction? Let them grow up and choose for themselves." Suppose some one had said to Jehosheba: "Don't interfere with that young Joash

Let him grow up and decide whether he likes the palace or not, whether he wants to be king or not. Don't disturb his volition." Jehosheba knew right well that unless that day the young king was rescued he would not be rescued at all.

I tell you, my friends, the reason we don't reclaim all our children from worldliness is because we begin too late. Parents wait until their children lie before they teach them the value of truth. They wait until their children swear before they teach them the importance of righteous conversation. They wait until their children are all wrapped up in this world before they tell them of a better world. Too late with your prayers. Too late with your discipline. Too late with your benediction. You put all care upon your children between 12 and 18. Why do you not put the chief care between 4 and 9? It is too late to repair a vessel when it has got out of the dry-dock! It is too late to save Joash after the executioners have broken in. May God arm us all for this work of snatching royal souls from death to coronation.

HOW PHOCUS DUG HIS GRAVE AND DIED.!

Can you imagine any sublimer work than this soul-saving? That was what flushed Paul's cheek with enthusiasm; that was what led Munson to risk his life amid Bornesian cannibals; that was what sent Dr. Abeel to preach under the consuming skies of China; that was what gave courage to Phocus in the third century. When the military officers came to put him to death for Christ's sake he put them to bed that they might rest while he himself went out and in his own garden dug his grave and then came back and said: "I am ready." But they were shocked at the idea of taking the life of their host. He said: "It is the will of God that I should die," and he stood on the margin of his own grave and they beheaded him. You say it is a mania, a foolhardiness, a fanaticism. Rather would I call it a glorious self-abnegation, the thrill of eternal satisfaction, the plucking of Joash from death and raising him to coronation.

THE CHURCH IS A GOOD HIDING PLACE.

The third thought I hand to you from my text is that the church of God is a good hiding-place. When Jehosheba rushes into the nursery of the king and picks up Joash what shall she do with him? Shall she take him to some room in the palace? No; for the official desperadoes will hunt through every nook and corner of that building. Shall she take him to the residence of some wealthy citizen? No; that citizen would not dare to harbor the fugitive. But she has to take him somewhere. She hears the cry of the mob in the streets; she hears the shriek of the dying nobility; so she rushes with Joash into the room of the temple, into the house of God, and then she puts him down. She knows that Athaliah and her wicked assassins will not bother the temple a great deal; they are not apt to go very much to church, and so she sets down Joash in the temple. There he will be hearing the songs of the worshipers year after year; there he will breathe the odor of the golden censers; in that sacred spot he will tarry, secreted until the six years have passed and he come to enthronement.

Would to God we were as wise as Jehosheba, and knew that the church of God is the best hiding-place. Perhaps our parents took us there in early days; they snatched us away from the world and hide us behind the baptismal fonts and amid the bibles and the psalm books. O glorious inclosure! We have been breathing

JESUS AND THE DOCTORS.

the breath of the golden censers all the time, and we have seen the lamb on the altar, and we have handled the phials which are the prayers of all saints, and we have dwelt under the wings of the cherubim. Glorious inclosure! When my father and my mother died, and the property was settled up, there was hardly anything left; but they endowed us with a property worth more than any earthly possession, because they hid us in the temple. And when days of temptation have come upon my soul I have gone there for shelter; and when assaulted of sorrows I have gone there for comfort, and there I mean to live. I want, like Joash, to stay there until coronation. I mean to be buried out of the house of God.

Oh, men of the world outside there, betrayed, caricatured, and cheated of the world, why do you not come in through the broad, wide-open door of Christian communion? I wish I could act the part of Jehosheba to-day, and steal you away from your perils and hide you in the temple. How few of us appreciate the fact that the church of God is a hiding-place. There are many people who put the church at so low a mark that they begrudge it everything, even the few dollars they give toward it. They make no sacrifices. They dole a little out of their surplusage. They pay their butcher's bill, and they pay their doctor's bill, and they pay their landlord, and they pay everybody but the lord, and they come in at the last to pay the Lord in his church, and frown as they say: "There, Lord, it is if you will have it, take it—now take it, take it; send me a receipt in full, and don't bother me soon again!"

I tell you there is not more than one man out of a thousand who appreciates what the church is. Where are the souls that put aside one-tenth for Christian institutions—one-tenth of their incomes? Where are those who, having put aside that one-tenth, draw upon it cheerfully? Why, it is to pull, and drag, and hold on, and grab, and clutch; and giving is an affliction to most people when it ought to be an exhilaration and a rapture. Oh, that God would remodel our souls on this subject and that we might appreciate the house of God as a great refuge. If your children are to come up to lives of virtue and happiness they will come up under the shade of the church. If the church does not get them the world will.

SAVE YOUR CHILDREN.

Ah, when you pass away—and it will not be long before you do—when you pass away it will be a satisfaction to see your children in Christian society. You want to have them sitting at the holy sacraments. You want them mingling in Christian associations. You would like to have them die in the sacred precints. When you are on your dying bed, and your little ones come up to take your last word, and you look into their bewildered faces, you will want to leave them under the church's benediction. I don't care how hard you are, that is so. I said to a man of the world: "Your son and daughter are going to join our church next Sunday. Have you any objections?" "Bless you," he said, "objections? I wish all my children belonged to the church. I don't attend to those matters myself—I am very wicked—but I am very glad they are going, and I shall be there to see them. I am very glad, sir; I am very glad. I want them there." And so, though you may have been wanderers from God, and though you may have sometimes caricatured the church of Jesus, it is your great desire that your sons and daughters should be standing all their lives within this sacred inclosure.

More than that, you yourself will want the church for a hiding place when the mortgage is foreclosed; when your daughter, just blooming into womanhood, suddenly clasps her hands in a slumber that knows no waking; when gaunt trouble walks through the parlor, and the sitting-room, and the dining-hall, and the nursery, you will want some shelter from the tempest. Ah, some of you have been run upon by misfortune and trial; why do you not come into the shelter? I said to a widowed mother after she had buried her only son— months after I said to her: "How do you get along nowadays?" "Oh," she replied, "I get along tolerable well except when the sun shines." I said: "What do you mean by that?" She said: "I can't bear to see the sun shine; my heart is so dark that all the brightness of the natural world seems a mockery to me." Oh, darkened soul, oh, broken-hearted man, broken-hearted woman, why do you not come into the shelter? I swing the door wide open. I swing it from wall to wall. Come in! Come in! You want a place where your troubles shall be interpreted, where your burdens shall be unstrapped, where your tears shall be wiped away.

Church of God, be a hiding place to all these people. Give them a seat where they can rest their weary souls. Flash some light from your chandeliers upon their darkness. With some soothing hymn hush their griefs. Oh, church of God, gate of heaven, let me go through it! All other institutions are going to fail; but the church of God—its foundation is the "Rock of Ages," its charter is for everlasting years, its keys are held by the universal proprietor, its dividend is heaven, its president is God!

"Sure as thy truth shall last,
To Zion shall be given
The brghtest glories earth can yield,

And brighter bliss of heaven."
God grant that all this audience, the youngest, the eldest, the worst, the best, may find their safe and glorious hiding place where Joash found it—in the temple!

ABRAHAM OEFEEING HIS SON ISAAC. (166)

IN LONDON.

SALVATION BY FAITH.

[Delivered in London, England, Jan., 19th., 1890.]
"*Believe on the Lord Jesus Christ and thou shalt be saved*". *Acts. xvi, 31.*

STANDING IN THE PHILIPPIAN DUNGEON!

AILS are dark, dull, damp, loathsome places even now, but they were worse in the apostolic times. I imagine today we are standing in the Philippian dungeon. Do you not feel the chill? Do you not hear the groan of those incarcerated ones who for ten years have not seen the sunlight and the deep sigh of women who remember their father's house and mourn over their wasted estates? Listen again. It is the cough of a consumptive or the struggle of one in a nightmare of a great horror. You listen again and hear a culprit, his chains rattling as he rolls over in his dreams, and you say: "God pity the prisoner." But there is another sound in that prison. It is a song of gladness. What a place to sing in! The music comes winding through the corridors of the prison, and in all the dark wards the whisper is heard: "What's that? What's that?,' It is the song of Paul and Silas. They cannot sleep. They have been whipped, very badly whipped. The long gashes on their backs are bleeding yet. They lie flat on the cold ground, their feet fast in wooden sockets; and of course they can not sleep. But they can sing.

Jailer, what are you doing with these people? Why have they been put in here?

Oh, they have been trying to make the world better.

Is that all?

That is all.

A pit for Joseph.

A lion's cave for Daniel. A blazing furnace for Shadrach. Clubs for John Wesley. An anathema for Philip Melanchton. A dungeon for Paul and Silas.

But while we are standing in the gloom of the Philippian dungeon, and we hear the mingling voices of sob, and groan, and blasphemy, and hallelujah, suddenly an earthquake! The iron bars of the prison twist, the pillars crack off, the solid masonry begins to heave and rock till all the doors swing open, and the walls fall with a terrific crash. The jailer, feeling himself responsible for these prisoners! and feeling suicide to be honorable—since Brutus killed himself, and Cato killed himself, and Cassius killed himself—puts his sword to his own heart, proposing with one strong, keen thrust

SALVATION BY FAITH. 109

to put an end to his excitement and agitation. But Paul cries out: "Stop! stop! Do thyself no harm. We are all here." Then I see the jailer running through the dust and amid the ruin of that prison, and I see him throwing himself down at the feet of these prisoners, crying out: "What shall I do? What shall I do?' Then Paul answers: "Get out of this place before there is another earthquake; put handcuffs and hobbles on these other prisoners lest they get away." No word of that kind. Compact, thrilling, tremendous answer; answer memorable all through earth and heaven: "Believe on the Lord Jesus Christ and thou shalt be saved."

THE CRASH OF EARTHQUAKES.

Well, we have all read of the earthquake in Lisbon, in Lima, in Aleppo, and in Caraccas, but we live in a latitude where in all our memory there has not been one severe volcanic disturbance. And yet we have seen fifty earthquakes. Here is a man who has been building up a large fortune. His bid on the money market was felt in all the cities. He thinks he has got beyond all annoying rivalries in trade and he says to himself: "Now I am free and safe from all possible perturbation." But a national panic strikes the foundations of the commercial world and crash! goes all the magnificent business establishment. He is a man who has built up a very beautiful home. His daughters have just come home from the seminary with diplomas of graduation. His sons have started in life, honest, temperate, and pure. When the evening lights are struck there is a happy and an unbroken family circle. But there has been an accident down at the beach. The young man ventured too far out in the surf. The telegraph hurled the terror up to the city. An earthquake struck under the foundation of that beautiful home. The piano closed; the curtains dropped; the laughter hushed. Crash! go all those domestic hopes and prospects and expectations. So, my friends, we have all felt the shaking down of some great trouble, and there was a time when we were as much excited as this man of the text, and we cried out as he did: "What shall I do? What shall I do?" The same reply that the apostle made to him is appropriate to us: "Believe on the Lord Jesus Christ and thou shalt be saved?"

THE SAVIORS NAME.

There are some documents of so little importance that you do not care to put any more than your last name under them, or even your initials, but there are some documents of so great importance that you write out your full name. So the Savior in some parts of the bible is called "Lord," and in other parts of the bible he is called "Jesus," and in other parts of the bible he is called "Christ," but that there might be no mistake about this passage all three names come in together— the "Lord Jesus Christ." Now, who is this being that you want me to trust in and believe in? Men sometimes come to me with credentials and certificates of good character; but I can not trust them. There is some dishonesty in their looks that makes me know I shall be cheated if I confide in them. You cannot put your heart's confidence in a man until you know what stuff he is made of, and am I reasonable this morning when I stop to ask you who this is that you want me to trust in? No man would think of venturing his life on a vessel going out to sea that had never been inspected. No, you must have the certificate hung amidships, telling how many tons it carries, and how long ago it was built, and who built it, and all about it.

And you can not expect me to risk the cargo of my immortal interests on board any craft till you tell me what it is made of, and where it was made, and what it is.

When, then, I ask you who this is you want me to trust in, you tell me he is a very attractive person. You tell me that the contemporary writers describe him, and they give the color of his eyes, and the color of his hair, and they describe his whole appearance as being resplendent. Christ did not tell the children to come to him. "Suffer little children to come unto me" was not spoken to the children; it was spoken to the Pharisees. The children had come without any invitation. No sooner did Jesus appear than the little ones pitched from their mothers' arms, an avalanche of beauty and love, into his lap. "Suffer little children to come unto me." That was addressed to the Pharisees; not to the children. Christ did not ask John to put his head down on his bosom; John could not help but put his head there. Such eyes, such cheeks, such a chin, such hair, such physical condition and appearance— why, it must have been completely captivating and winsome. I suppose a look at him was just to love him. Oh! how attractive his manner. Why, when they saw Christ coming along the street they ran into their houses, and they wrapped up their invalids as quick as they could, and brought them out that he might look at them. Oh! there was something so pleasant, so inviting, so cheering in everything he did, in his very look. When these sick ones were brought out did he say: "Take away these sores; do not trouble me with these leprosies?" No, no; there was a kind look, there was a gentle word, there was a healing touch. They could not keep away from him.

In addition to this softness of character, there was a fiery momentum. How the old hypocrites trembled before him. How the kings of the earth turned pale. Here is a plain man, with a few sailors at his back, coming off the sea of Galilee, going up to the palace of the Cæsars, making that palace quake to the foundations, and uttering a word of mêrcy and kindness which throbs through all the earth, and through all the heavens, and through all the ages. Oh! he was a loving Christ. But it was not effeminacy or insipidity of character; it was accompanied with majesty, infinite and omnipotent.

THE WONDROUS DEATH.

Lest the world should not realize his earnestness, this Christ mounts the cross. You say: "If Christ has to die, why not let him take some deadly potion and lie on a couch in some bright and beautiful home? If he must die, let him expire amid all kindly attentions." No, the world must hear the hammers on the heads of the spikes. The world must listen to the death-rattle of the sufferer. The world must feel his warm blood dropping on each cheek, while it looks up into the face of his anguish. And so the cross must be lifted and the hole is dug on the top of Calvary. It must be dug three feet deep, and then the cross is laid on the ground, and the sufferer is stretched upon it, and the nails are pounded through nerve, and muscle, and bone, through the right hand, through the left hand, and then they shake his right hand to see if it is fast and then they shake his left foot to see if it is fast, and then they heave up the wood, half a dozen shoulders under the weight, and they put the end of the cross to the mouth of the hole, and they plunge it in, all the weight of his body coming down for the first time on the spikes, and while some hold the cross upright others throw in the dirt and trample it down, and trample it hard. Oh, plant that tree well and thoroughly, for it is to bear fruit such as no other tree ever bore. Why did Christ endure it? He could have taken those rocks and with them crushed his crucifiers. He could have reached up and grasped the sword of the omnipotent God and with one clean cut have tumbled them into perdition. But no; he was to die. He must die. His life for my life. His life for your life.

A STORY OF A YOUNG MAN.

In one of the European cities a young man died on the scaffold for the crime of murder. Some time after the mother of this young man was dying and the priest came in, and she made a confession to the priest that she was the murderer, and not her son; in a moment of anger she had struck her husband a blow that slew him. The son came suddenly into the room and was washing away the wounds and trying to resuscitate his father when some one looked through the window and saw him and supposed him to be the criminal. That young man died for his own mother. You say: "It was wonderful that he never exposed her." But I tell you of a grander thing. Christ, the son of God, died, not for his mother, not for his father, but for his sworn enemies. Oh, such a Christ as that—so loving, so self-sacrificing—can you not trust him?

HOW TO TRUST CHRIST.

I think there are many under the spirit of God who are saying: "I will trust him if he will only tell me how," and the great question asked by thousands in this assemblage is: "How? How?" And while I answer your question I look up and utter the prayer which Rowland Hill so often uttered in the midst of his sermons: "Master, help!" How are you to trust in Christ? Just as you trust any one. You trust your partner in business with important things. If a commercial house give you a note payable three months hence you expect the payment of that note at the end of three months. You have perfect confidence in their word and in their ability. You go home to-day. You expect there will be food on the table. You have confidence in that. Now, I ask you to have the same confidence in the Lord Jesus Christ. He says: "You believe; I take away your sins," and they are all taken away. "What!" you say, "before I pray any more? Before I read my bible any more? Before I cry over my sins any more?" Yes, this moment. Believe with all your heart and you are saved.

Why, Christ is only waiting to get from you what you give to scores of people every day. What is that? Confidence. If these people whom you trust day by day are more worthy than Christ, if they are more faithful than Christ, if they have done more than Christ ever did, then give them the preference; but if you really think that Christ is as trustworthy as they are, then deal with him as fairly. "Oh!" says some one in a light way, "I believe that Christ was born in Bethlehem, and I believe that he died on the cross." Do you believe it with your head or your heart?

SAVING FAITH.

I will illustrate the difference. You are in your own house. In the morning you open a newspaper, and you read how Capt. Braveheart on the sea risked his life for the salvation of his passengers. You say: "What a grand fellow he must have been! His family deserves very well of the country." You fold the newspaper and sit down at the table, and perhaps do not think of that incident again. That is historical faith. But now you are on the sea, and it is night, and you are asleep, and are awakened by the shriek of "Fire!" You rush out on the deck. You hear, amid the wringing of the hands the fainting, the cries: "No hope! We are lost! we are lost!" The sail puts out its wings of fire, the ropes make a burning ladder in the night heavens, the spirit of wreck hisses in the waves, and on the hurricane deck shakes out its banner of smoke and darkness. "Down with the life boats!" cries the captain. "Down with the life boats!,' People rush into them. The boats are about full. Room only for one more man. You are standing on the deck beside the captain. Who shall it be? You or the captain? The captain says: "You." You jump and are saved. He stands there and dies. Now, you believe Capt. Braveheart sacrificed himself for his passengers, but you believe it with love, with tears, with hot and long continued exclamations, with grief at his loss and with joy at your deliverance. That is saving faith. In other words, what you believe with all the heart, and believe in regard to yourself. On this hinge turns my sermon; aye, the salvation of your immortal soul.

You often go across a bridge you know nothing about. You do not know who built the bridge, you do not know what material it is made of, but you come to it, and walk over it, and ask no questions. And here is an arched bridge, blasted from the "Rock of Ages" and built by the architect of the whole universe, spanning the dark gulf between sin and righteousness, and all God asks you is to walk across it, and you start, and you come to it, and you go a little way on, and you stop, and you fall back, and you experiment. You say: "How do I know that bridge will hold me?" instead of marching on with firm step, asking no questions, but feeling that the strength of the eternal God is under you.

Oh, was there ever a prize offered so cheap as pardon and heaven are offered to you? For how much? A million dollars? It is certainly worth more than that. But cheaper than that you can have it. Ten thousand dollars? Less than that. Five thousand dollars? Less than that. One dollar? Less than that. One farthing? Less than that. "Without money and without price." No money to pay. No journey to take. No penance to suffer. Only just one decisive action of the soul: "Believe in the Lord Jesus Christ and thou shalt be saved."

A HAPPY LIFE.

Shall I try to tell you what it is to be saved? I can not tell you. No man, no angel, can tell you. But I can hint at it. For my text brings me up to this point: "Thou shalt be saved." It means a happy life here, and a peaceful death and a blissful eternity. It is a grand thing to go to sleep at night, and to get up in the morning, and to do business all day, feeling that all is right between my heart and God. No accident, no sickness,, no persecution, no peril, no sword can do me any permanent damage. I am a forgiven child of God, and he is bound to see me through. He has sworn he will see me through. The mountains may depart, the earth may burn, the light of the stars may be blown out by the blast of the judgment hurricane, but life and death, things present and things to come are mine.

A PEACEFUL DEATH.

Yea, farther than that—it means a peaceful death.

Mrs. Hemans, Mrs. Sigourney, Dr. Young, and almost all the poets have said handsome things about death. There is nothing beautiful about it. When we stand by the white and rigid features of those whom we love and they give no answering pressure of the hand and no returning kiss of the lip, we do not want anybody poetizing around about us. Death is loathsomeness and midnight and the wringing of the heart until the tendrils snap and curl in the torture unless Christ be with us. I confess to you of an infinite fear, a consuming horror of death unless Christ shall be with me. I would rather go down into a cave of wild beasts or a jungle of reptiles than into the grave unless Christ goes with me. Will you tell me that I am to be carried out from my bright home and put away in the darkness? I cannot bear darkness. At the first coming of the evening I must have the gas lit, and the further on in life I get the more I like to have my friends around me. And am I to be put off for thousands of years in a dark place, with no one to speak to? When the holidays come and the gifts are distributed shall I add no joy to the "Merry Christmas" or the "Happy New Year?" Ah, do not point down to the hole in the ground, the grave, and call it a beautiful place; unless there be some supernatural illumination. I shudder back from it. My whole nature revolts at it.

But now this glorious lamp is lifted above the grave and all the darkness is gone and the way is clear. I look into it now without a single shudder. Now my anxiety is not about death; my anxiety is that I may live aright, for I know that if my life is consistent when I come to the last hour, and this voice is silent, and these eyes are closed, and these hands with which I beg for your eternal salvation to-day are folded over the still heart, that then I shall only begin to live. What power is there in anything to chill me in the last hour if Christ wraps around me the skirt of his own garment? What darkness can fall upon my eyelids then, amid the heavenly daybreak? O death, I will not fear thee then! Back to thy cavern of darkness, thou robber of all the earth. Fly, thou despoiler of families. With this battle-ax I hew thee in twain from helmet to sandal, the voice of Christ sounding all over the earth, and through the heavens: "O death, I will be thy plague. O grave, I will be thy destruction."

A BLISSFUL ETERNITY.

To be saved is to wake up in the presence of Christ. You know when Jesus was on earth how happy he made every house he went into, and when he brings us up to his house how great our glee. His voice has more music in it than is to be heard in all the oratorios of eternity. Talk not about banks dasked with efflorescence. Jesus is the chief bloom of heaven. We shall see the very face that beamed sympathy in Bethany and take the very hand that dropped its blood from the short beam of the the cross. Oh, I want to stand in eternity with him. Toward that harbor I steer. Toward that goal I run. I shall be satisfied when I awake in his likeness. Oh, broken-hearted men and women, how sweet it will be in that good land to pour all your hardships, and bereavements and losses, into the loving ear of Christ, and then have him explain why it was best for you to be sick, and why it was best for you to be widowed, and why it was best for you to be persecuted, and why it was best for you to be tried, and have him point to an elevation proportionate to your disquietude here, saying: "You suffered with me on earth, come up now and be glorified with me in heaven."

A MOTHERS STORY.

Some one went into a house where there had been a good deal of trouble and said to the woman there: "You seem to be lonely." "Yes," she said, "I am lonely." "How many in family?" "Only myself." "Have you had any children?" "I had seven children." "Where are they?" "Gone." "All gone?" "All." "All dead?" Then she breathed a long sigh into the loneliness, and said: "Oh, sir, I have been a good mother to the grave." And so there are hearts here that are utterly broken down by the bereavements of life. I point you today to the eternal balm of heaven. Are there any here that I am missing this morning? Oh you good waiting-maid! your heart's sorrow poured in no human ear, lonely and sad! how glad you will be when Christ shall disband all your sorrows and crown you queen unto God and the lamb forever! O aged men and women, fed by his love and warmed by his grace for three-score years and ten! will not your decrepitude change for the leap of a hart when you come to look face to face upon him whom, having not seen, you love? Oh, that will be the good shepherd, not out in the night and watching to keep off the wolves, but with the lambs reclining on the sunlit hill! That will be the captain of our salvation, not amid the roar, and crash, and boom of battle, but amid the disbanded troop keeping victorious festivity. That will be the bridegroom of the church coming from the altar, the bride leaning upon his arm while he looks down into her face and says: "Behold, thou art fair, my love! Behold, thou art fair!"

JERUSALEM.

IN QUEENSTOWN, IRELAND.

"*For of such is the Kingdom of Heaven.*"

THE NAME OF JESUS.

[Delivered at Queenstown, Ireland, Jan., 29th, 1890.]

"*A name which is above every name.*" Philippians, ii, 9.

A GOOD NAME.

ON MY way from the Holy land, and while I wait for the steamer to resume her voyage to America, I preach to you from this text, which was one of Paul's rapturous and enthusiastic descriptions of the name of Jesus. By common proverb we have come to believe that there is nothing in a name, and so parents sometimes present their children for baptism regardless of the title given them, and not thinking that that particular title will be either a hindrance or a help. Strange mistake. You have no right to give to your child a name that is lacking either in euphony or in moral meaning. It is a sin for you to call your child Jehoiakims or Tiglath-Pileser. Because you yourself may have an exasperating name is no reason why you should give it to those who come after you. But how often we have seen some name, filled with jargon, rattling down from generation to generation, simply because some one a long while ago happened to be afflicted with it Institutions and enterprises have sometimes without sufficient deliberation taken their nomenclature. Mighty destinies have been decided by the significance of a name. There are men who all their life long toil and tussle to get over the influence of some unfortunate name. While we may, through right behavior and Christian demeanor, outlive the fact that we were baptized by the name of a despot, or an infidel, or a cheat, how much better it would have been if we all could have started life without any such incumbrance. When I find the apostle, in my text and in other parts of his writing, breaking out in dsecriptions of admiration in regard to the name of Jesus, I want to inquire what are some of the characteristics of that appellation. And O that the Saviour himself, while I speak, might fill me with his own presence, for we never can tell to others that which we have not ourselves felt.

AN EASY NAME.

First, this name of Jesus is an easy name. Sometimes we are introduced to people whose name is so long and unpronounceable that we have sharply to listen, and to hear the name given to us two or three times, before we venture to speak it. But within the first two years the little child clasps its hands, and looks up, and says "Jesus." Can it be, amid all the families represented here today, there is one household where the little ones speak of "father," and "mother," and "brother," and "sister," and not of "the name which is above every name?" Sometimes we forget the titles of our best friends, and we have to pause and think before we can recall the name. But can you imagine any freak of intellect in which you could forget the Saviour's designation? That word "Jesus" seems to fit the tongue in every dialect. When the voice in old age gets feeble and tremulous, and indistinct, still this regal word has potent utterance.

> Jesus, I love Thy charming name,
>   Tis music to my ear;
> Fain would I sound it out so loud
>   That heaven and earth might hear.

A BEAUTIFUL NAME.

Still further, I remark it is a beautiful name. You have noticed that it is impossible to disassociate a name from the person who has the name. So there are names that are to me repulsive—I do not want to hear them at all—while those very names are attractive to you. Why the difference? It is because I happen to know persons by those names who are cross, and sour, and snappish, and queer, while the persons you used to know by those names were pleasant and attractive. As we cannot dissociate a name from the person who holds the name, that consideration makes Christ's name so unspeakably beautiful. No sooner is it pronounced in your presence than you think of Bethlehem, and Gethsemane, and Golgotha, and you see the loving face, and hear the tender voice, and feel the gentle touch. You see Jesus, the one who, though banquetting with heavenly hierarches, came down to breakfast on the fish that rough men had just hauled out of Genessaret;

Jesus, the one who, though the clouds are the dust of his feet, walked footsore on to the road to Emmaus.

Just as soon as that name is pronounced in your presence you think of how the shining one gave back the centurion's daughter, and how he helped the blind man to the sunlight, and how he made the cripple's crutches useless, and how he looked down into the babe's laughing eyes, and, as the little one struggled to go to him, flung out his arms around it, and impressed a loving kiss on its brow, and said: "Of such is the kingdom of heaven." Beautiful name—Jesus! It stands for love, for patience, for kindness, for forbearance, for self sacrifice, for magnanimity. It is aromatic with all odors and accordant with all harmônies. Sometimes I see that name, and the letters seem to be made out of tears, and then again they look like gleaming crowns. Sometimes they seem to as though twisted out of the straw on which he lay, and then as though built out of the thrones on which his people shall reign. Sometimes I sound that word "Jesus," and I hear coming through the two syllables the sigh of Gethsemane and the groan of Calvary; and again I sound it, and it is all a-ripple with gladness and a-ring with hosanna. Take all the glories of book bindery and put them around the page where that name is printed. On Christmas morning wreathe it on the wall.

Let it drip from the harp's strings and thunder out in organ's diapasom. Sound it often, sound it well, until every star shall seem to shine it, and every flower shall seem to breathe it, and mountain and sea, and day and night, and earth and heaven acclaim in full chant: "Blessed be his glorious name forever; The name that is above every mame."

        Jesus, the name high over all,
        In heaven and earth and sky.

To the repenting soul, to the exhausted invalid, to the to the Sunday school girl, to the snow white octogenarian, it is beautiful. The old man comes in from a long walk, and tremblingly opens the door, and hangs his hat on the old nail, and sets his cane in the usual corner, and lies down on a couch, and says to his children and grandchildren: "My dears, I am going to leave you." They say: "Why, where are you going, grandfather?" "I am going to Jesus." And so the old man faints away into heaven. The little child comes in from play and throws herself on your lap, and says; "Mamma, I am so sick, I am so sick." And you put her to bed, and the fever is worse and worse, until in some midnight she looks up into your face and says; "Mamma, kiss me good-by, I am going away from you." And you say: "My dear, where are you going to?" And she says: "I am going to Jesus." And the red cheeks which you thought was the mark of the fever, only turns out to be the carnation bloom of heaven. Oh yes; it is a sweet name spoken by the lips of childhood, spoken by the old man.

A MIGHTY NAME.

Still further it is a mighty name. Rothchild is a potent name in the commercial world, Cuvier in the scientific, Irving a powerful name in the literary world, Washington an influential name in the political world Wellington a mighty name in the military world, but tell me any name in all the earth so potent to awe, and lift, and thrill, and rouse. and agitate, and bless, as this name of Jesus. That one word unhorsed Saul, and flung Newton on his face on ship's deck, and today holds 400,000,000 of the race with omnipotent spell. That name in England today means more than Victoria: in Germany, means more than Emperor William; in

THE NAME OF JESUS.

France, means more than Carnot; in Italy, means more than Hubert of the present or Garibaldi of the past. I have seen a man bound hand foot in sin, satan his hard task master, in a bondage from which no human power could deliver him, and yet at the pronunciation of that one word he dashed down his chains and marched out forever free. I have seen a man overwhelmed with disaster, the last hope fled, the last light gone out; that name pronounced in his hearing, the sea dropped, the clouds scattered, and a sunburst of eternal gladness poured into his soul. I have seen a man hardened in infidelity, defiant of God, full of scoff and jeer, jocose of the judgment, reckless of an unending eternity, at the mere pronunciation of that namd blanch, and cower, and quake, and pray, and sob, and moan, and believe, and rejoice.

Oh, it is a mighty name! At its utterance the last wall of sin will fall, the last temple of superstition crumble, the last juggernaut of cruelty crash to pieces. That name will first make all the earth tremble, and then it will make all the nations sing. It is to be the password of every gate of honor, the insignia on every flag, the shout in every conflict. All the millions of the earth are to know it. The red horse of carnage seen in apocalyptic vision and the black horse of death, are to fall back on their haunches, and the white horse of victory will go forth, mounted by him who hath the moon under his feet, and the stars of heaven for his tiara. Other dominions seem to be giving out; this seems to be enlarging. Spain has had to give up much of her dominion. Austria has been wonderfully depleted in power. France has had to surrender some of her favorite provinces. Most of the thrones of the world are being lowered, and most of the sceptres of the world are being shortened; but every Bible printed, every tract distributed, every Sunday school class taught, every school founded, every church established, is extending the power of Christ's name. That name has hardly been spoken under the Chinese wall, and in Siberian snow castle, in Brazilian grove and in eastern pagoda. That name is to swallow up all other names. That crown is to cover up all other crowns. That empire is to absorb all other dominations.

> All crimes shall cease, and ancient frauds shall fail,
> Returning justice lift aloft her scale;
> Peace o'er the world her olive wand extend,
> And white robed innocence from heaven descend.

AN ENDURING NAME.

Still further: it is an enduring name. You clamber over the fence of the graveyard and pull aside the weeds, and you see the faded inscription on the tombstone. That was the name of a man who once ruled all that town. The mightiest names of the world have either perished or are perishing. Gregory VI, Sancho of Spain, Conrad I, of Germany, Richard I, of England, Louis XVI, of France, Catharine of Russia—mighty names once, that made the world tremble; but now, none so poor as to do them reverence, and to the great mass of people they mean absolutely nothing; they never heard of them. But the name of Christ is to endure forever.

It will be perpetuated in art, for there will be other Bellinis to depict the Madonna; there will be other Ghirlandaios to represent Christ's baptism; there will be other Bronzinos to show us Christ visiting the spirits in prison; other Giottos to appall our sight with the crucifixion.

The name will be preserved in song, for there will be other Alexander Popes to write the "Messiah," other Dr. Youngs to portray his triumph, other Cowpers to sing his love. It will be preserved in costly and magnificent architecture, for, Protestantism as well as Catholicism is yet to have its St. Marks and its St. Peters.

That name will be preserved in the literature of the world, for already it is embalmed in the best books, and there will be other Dr. Paleys to write the "evidences of Christianity," and other Richard Baxters to describe the Saviour's coming to judgment.

But above all, and more than all, that name will be embalmed in the memory of all the good of earth and all the great ones of heaven. Will the delivered bondman of earth ever forget who freed him? Will the blind man of earth forget who gave him sight? Will the outcast of earth forget who brought him home? No! No!

To destroy the memory of that name of Christ, you would have to burn up all the Bibles and all the churches on earth, and then in a spirit of universal arson go through the gate of heaven, and put a torch to the temples and the towers and the palaces, and after all that city was wrapped in awful conflagration, and the citizens came out and gazed on the ruin—even then, they would hear that name in the thunder of falling tower and the crash of crumbling wall, and see it inwrought in the flying banners of flame, and the redeemed of the Lord on high would be happy yet and cry out: "Let the palaces and temples burn, we have Jesus left!" "Blessed be his glorious name for ever and ever. The name that is above every name."

WHAT NAME WILL YOU CALL CHRIST.

Have you ever made up your mind by what name you will call Christ when you meet him in heaven? You know he has many names. Will you call him Jesus, or the Annointed One, or the Messiah, or will you take some of the symbolical names which on earth you learned from your Bible?

Wandering some day in the garden of God on high, the place a-bloom with eternal springtide, infinite, luxuriance of rose, and lily, and amaranth, you may look up into his face and say: "My Lord, thou art the rose of Sharon and the lily of the valley."

Some day, as a soul comes up from earth to take its place in the firmament, and shine as a star for ever and ever, and the luster of a useful life shall beam forth tremulous and beautiful, you may look up into the face of Christ and say: "My Lord, thou art a brighter star—the morning star—a star forever."

Wandering some day amid the fountains of life that toss in the sunlight and fall in crash of peal and amethyst in golden and crystaline urn, and you wander up the round banked river to where it first tingles its silver on the rock, and out of the chalices of love you drink to honor and everlasting joy, you may look up into the face of Christ and say: "My Lord, thou art the fountain of living water."

Some day, wandering amid the lambs and sheep in the heavenly pastures, feeding by the rock, rejoicing in the presence of him who brought you out of the wolfish wilderness to the sheepfold above, you may look up into his loving and watchful eye and say: "My Lord, thou art the shepherd of the everlasting hills."

But there is another name you may select. I will imagine that heaven is done. Every throne has its king. Every harp has its harper. Heaven has gathered up everything that is worth having. The treasures of the whole universe have poured into it. The song full. The ranks full. The mansions full. Heaven full. The sun shall set afire with splendor the domes of the temples and burnish the golden streets into a blaze

SYMBOL OF THE NEW DISPENSATION.

and be reflected back from the solid pearl of the twelve gates and it shall be noon in heaven, noon on the river, noon on the hills noon in all the valleys—high noon. Then the soul may look up gradually accustoming itself to the vision, shading the eyes as from the almost insufferable splendor of the noonday light, until the vision can endure it, then crying out: "Thou art the sun that never sets!

At this point I am staggered with the thought that notwithstanding all the charm in the name of Jesus, and the fact that it is so easy a name, and so beautiful a name, and so potent a name, and so enduring a name, there are people who find no charm in those two syllables.

O COME THIS DAY TO CHRIST.

O come this day and see whether there is anything in Jesus. I challenge those of you who are farther from God to come at the close of this service and test with me whether God is good, and Christ is gracious, and the Holy Spirit is omnipotent. I challenge you to come and kneel down with me at the altar of mercy. I will kneel on one side of the altar and you kneel on the other side of it, and neither of us will rise until our sins are forgiven, and we ascribe, in the words of the text, all honor to the name of Jesus—you pronouncing it, I pronouncing it—the nâme that is above every name.

> His worth if all the nations knew,
> Sure the whole earth would love him too.

O that God today, by the power of his holy spirit, would roll over you a vision of that blessed Christ, and you would begin to weep and pray and believe and rejoice. You have heard of the warrior who went out to fight against Christ. He knew he was in the wrong, while waging the war against the kingdom of Christ;

THE NAME OF JESUS.

an arrow struck him and he fell. It pierced him in the heart, and lying there, his face to the sun, his life blood running away, he caught a handful of the blood that was rushing out in his right hand, and held it up before the sun and cried out: "O Jesus thou hast conquered!" And if today the arrow of God's spirit piercing your soul, you felt the truth of what I have been trying to proclaim, you would surrender now and forever to the Lord who bought you. Glorious name! I know not whether you will accept it or not; but I will tell you one thing here and now, in the presence of angels and men, I take him to be my Lord, my God, my pardon' my peace, my life, my joy, my salvation, my heaven. "Blessed be his glorious name forever. The name that is above every name." "Hallelujah! unto him that sitteth upon the throne and unto the lamb forever and ever! Amen and amen and amen."

RAHAB CONCEALING THE SPIES.

HOME AGAIN.

THE HOUSE ON THE WALL.
[Delivered in Brooklyn, N. Y., February, 9th., 1890.]

"And the young men that were spies, went in and brought out Rahab, and her father, and her mother, and her brethren, and all that she had." Joshua, vi, 23.

WHEN, only a few weeks ago, I visited Jericho, I said, can it be possible that this dilapidated place is the Jericho that Mark Antony gave as a wedding present to Cleopatra? Where are the groves of palm trees? Where are Herod's palaces which once stood here? Where is the great theatre from the stage of which Salome told the people that Herod was dead? Where is the sycamore tree on the limb of which Zaccheus sat when Jesus passed this place? Where is the wreck of the walls that fell at the blowing of the rams' horns? But the fact that all these have disappeared did not hinder me from seeing in imagination the smash of everything on that fated day, save one house on the wall. The scene centuries ago comes back to me as though it were yesterday.

A SAD HOUSE.

There is a very sick and sad house in the city of Jericho. What is the matter? Is it poverty? No. Worse than that. Is it leprosy? No. Worse than that. Is it death? No. Worse than that. A daughter has forsaken her home. By what infernal plot she was induced to leave I know not; but they look in vain for her return. Sometimes they hear a footstep very much like hers' and they start up and say: "She comes!" but only to sink back again into disappointment. Alas! Alas! The father sits by the hour, with his face in his hands, saying not one word. The mother's hair is becoming gray too fast, and she begins to stoop so that those who saw her only a little while ago in the street know her not now as she passes. The brothers clench their fists, swearing vengeance against the despoiler of their home. Alas! will the poor soul never come back? There is a long, deep shadow over all the household. Added to this there is an invading army six miles away, just over the river, coming on to destroy the city; and what with the loss of their child and the coming on of that destructive army, I think the old people wished that they could die. That is the first scene in this drama of the Bible.

TWO SPIES.

In a house on the wall of the city is that daughter. That is her home now. Two spies have come from the invading army to look around through Jericho and see how best it may be taken. Yonder is the lost child, in that dwelling on the wall of the city. The police hear of it, and soon there is the shuffling of feet all around about the door, and the city government demands the surrender of those two spies. First, Rahab—for that was the name of the lost child—First, Rahab secretes the two spies and gets their pursuers off the track, but after awhile she says to them: "I will make a bargain with you. I will save your life if you will save my life, and the life of my father and my mother, and my brothers, and my sisters, when the victorious army comes upon the city." O, she had not forgotten her home yet, you see. The wanderer never forgets home. Her heart breaks now as she thinks of how she has maltreated her parents, and she wishes she were back with them again, and she wishes she could get away from her sinful enthrallment; and sometimes she looks up in the face of the midnight, bursting into agonizing tears. No sooner have these two spies promised to save her life, and the life of her father, and mother, and brothers, and sisters, than Rahab takes a scarlet cord and ties it around the body of one of the spies, brings him to the window, and as he clambers out—nervous lest she have not strength to hold him—with muscular arms such as as woman seldom has, she lets him down, hand over hand, in safety to the ground. Not being exhausted, she ties the cord around the other spy, brings him to the window, and just as successfully lets him down to the ground. No sooner have these men untied the scarlet cord from their bodies than they look up, and they say: "You had better get all your friends in this house —your father, your mother, your brothers and your sisters; you had better get them in this house. And then, after you have them here, take this red cord which you have put around our bodies and tie it across the window, and when our victorious army comes up, and sees that scarlet thread in the window, they will spare this house and all who are in it. Shall it be so?"

cried the spies. "Aye, aye," said Rahab, from the window, "it shall be so." That is the second scene in this Bible drama.

FLY! FLY!

There is a knock at the door of the old man. He looks up and says: "Come in," and lo! there is Rahab, the lost child; but she has no time to talk. They gather in excitement around her, and she says to them: "Get ready quickly, and go with me to my house. The army is coming! The trumpet! Make haste! Fly! The enemy"! That is the third scene in this Bible drama.

The hosts of Israel are all around about the doomed city of Jericho. Crash goes the great metropolis, heaps on heaps. The air suffocating with the dust, and horrible with the screams of a dying city. All the houses flat down. All the people dead. Ah no, no. On a crag of the wall—the only piece of the wall left standing—there is a house which we must enter. There is a family there that have been spared. Who are they? Let us go and see. Rahab, her father, her mother, her brothers, her sisters, all safe, and the only house left standing in all the city. What saved them? Was the house more firmly built? Oh, no; it was built in the most perilous place—on the wall; and the wall was the first thing that fell. Was it because her character was any better than any of the other population of the city? O, no. Why, then, was she spared and all her household? Can you tell me why? O, it was the scarlet line in the window. That is the fourth scene in this Bible drama.

THE SCARLET THREAD.

When the destroying angel went through Egypt it was the blood of the lamb on the door posts that saved the Israelites; and now that vengeance has come upon

PLAINS OF JERICHO.

Jericho it is the same color that assures the safety of Rahab and all her household. My friends, there are foes coming upon us, more deadly and more tremendous, to overthrow our immortal interests. They will trample us down and crush us out forever, unless there be some skillful mode of rescue open. The police of death already begin to clamor for our surrender; but, blessed be God, there is a way out. It is through the window, and by a rope so saturated with the blood of the cross that it is as red as that with which the spies were lowered; and if once our souls are delivered, then the scarlet cord stretched across the window of our escape, we may defy all bombardment, earthly and satanic.

STRETCH THIS SCARLET CORD.

In the first place, carrying out the idea of my text, we must stretch this scarlet cord across the window of rescue. There comes a time when a man is surrounded. What is that in the front door of his soul? It is the threatenings of the future. What is that in the back door of the soul? It is the sins of the past. He cannot get out of either of those doorways. If he attempts it he will be cut to pieces. What shall he do? Escape through the window of God's mercy. That sunshine has been pouring in for many a day. God's inviting mercy. God's pardoning mercy. God's all conquering mercy. God's everlasting mercy. But you say the window is so high. Ah, there is a rope, the very one with which the cross and its victim were lifted. That was strong enough to hold Christ, and it is strong enough to hold you. Bear all your weight upon it, all your hopes for this life, all your hopes for the life that is to come. Escape now through the window.

"But," you say, "that cord is too small to save me; that salvation will never do at all for such a sinner as

I have been." I suppose that the rope with which Rahab let the two spies to the ground was not thick enough: but they took that or nothing. And, my dear brother, that is your alternative. There is only one scarlet line that can save you. There have been hundreds and thousands who have been borne away in safety by that scarlet line, and it will bear you away in safety. Do you notice what a very narrow escape those two spies had? I suppose they came with flustered cheek and with excited heart. They had a very narrow escape. They went in the broad door of sin; but how did they come out? They came out of the window. They went up by the stairs of stone; they came down on a slender thread. And so, my friends, we go easily and unabashedly into sin, and all the doors are open; but if we get out at all it will be by being let down over precipices, wriggling and helpless, the strong grip above keeping us from being dashed on the rocks beneath. It is easy to get into sin, young man. It is not so easy to get out of it.

THE FIRST STEP.

A young man goes to the marble counter of a hotel. He asks for a brandy smash—called so, I suppose, because it smashes the man that takes it. There is no intoxication in it. As the young man receives it he does not seem to be at all excited. It does not give any glossiness to the eye. He walks home in beautiful apparel, and all his prospects are brilliant. That drink is not going to destroy him, but it is the first step on a bad road. Years have passed on, and I see that young man after he has gone the whole length of dissipation. It is midnight, and he is in a hotel—perhaps the very one where he took the first drink. A delirium is on him. He rises from the bed and comes to the window, and it is easily lifted; so he lifts it. Then he pushes back the blinds and puts his foot on the window-sill. Then he gives one spring, and the watchman finds his disfigured body, unrecognizable, on the pavement. O, if he had only waited a little while—if he had come down on the scarlet ladder that Jesus holds from the wall for him, and for you, and for me; but no, he made one jump, and was gone.

A minister of Christ was not long ago dismissed from his diocese for intoxication, and in a public meeting he gave this account of his sorrow; He said: "I had a beautiful home once; but strong drink shattered it. I had beautiful children; but this fiend of rum took their dimpled hands in his and led them to the grave. I had a wife—to know her was to love her; but she sits in wretchedness to-night, while I wander over the earth. I had a mother, and the pride of her life was I; but the thunderbolt struck her. I now have scarcely a friend in the world. Taste of the bitter cup I have tasted, and then answer me as to whether I have any hatred for the agency of my ruin. Hate it? I hate the whole damning traffic. I would to God to-night that every distillery was in flames, for then in the glowing sky I would write in the smoke of the ruin: "Woe to him that putteth the bottle to his neighbor's lips!" That minister of the gospel went in through the broad door of temptation; he came out of the window. And when I see the temptations that are about us in all countries, and when I know the proclivities to sin in every man's heart, I see that if any of us escape it will be a very narrow escape. O, if we have, my friends, got off from our sin, let us tie the scarlet thread by which we have been saved across the window. Let us do it in praise of him whose blood dyed it that color. Let it be in announcement of the fact that we shall no more be fatally assaulted. "There is now no condemnation to them that are in Jesus Christ." Then let all the forces of this world come up in cavalry charge, and let spirits of darkness come on—an infernal storming party attempting to take our soul—this rope twisted from these words. "The blood of Jesus Christ cleanseth from all sin," will hurl them back defeated forever.

PROTECT YOUR HOUSEHOLD.

Still further, we must take this red cord of the text and stretch it across the window of our households. When the Israelitish army came up against Jericho, they said: "What is that in the window?" Some one said: "That is a scarlet line." "Oh," said some one else, "that must be the house that was to be spared. Don't touch it." That line was thick enough, and long enough, and conspicuous enough to save Rahab, her father, her mother, her brothers and her sisters—the entire family. Have our households as good protection? You have bolts on the front door and on the back, and fastenings to the window, and perhaps burglar alarms, and perhaps an especial watchman blowing his whistle at midnight before your dwelling; but all that cannot protect your household. Is there on our houses the sign of a Saviour's sacrifice and mercy? Is there a scarlet line in the window? Have your children been consecrated to Christ? Have you been washed in the blood of the atonement? In what room do you have family prayers? Show me where it is you are accustomed to kneel. The sky is black with the coming deluge. Is your family inside or outside of the ark? It is a sad thing for a man to reject Christ: but to lie down and in the night of sin, across the path of heaven, so that his family come up and trip over him—that is terrific. It is a sad thing for a mother to reject Christ; but to gather her family around her, aud then take them by the hand and lead them out into the paths of worldliness, away from God and heaven, alas! alas! There may be geranium and cactus in that family window, and upholstery hovering over it, and childish faces looking out of it, but there is no scarlet thread stretched across it. Although that house may seem to be on the best street in all the town or city, it is really on the edge of a marsh, across which sweep poisonous malarias and it has a sandy foundation, and its splendor will come down, and great will be the fall of it. A home without God! A prayerless father! An undevout mother! Awful! Awful! Is that you? Will you keep on, my brother, on the wrong road, and take your loved ones with you? Time is so short that we cannot waste any of it in apologies, or indirections, circumlocutions. You owe to your children, O father, O mother, more than food, more than clothing, more than shelter—you owe them the example of a prayerful, consecrated, pronounced, out and out Christian life. You cannot afford to keep it away from them.

MY GOOD MOTHER.

Now, as I stand here, you do not see any hand outstretched towards me, and yet there are hands on both my shoulders. They are hands of parental benediction. It is quite a good many years ago now since we folded those hands as they began their last sleep on the banks of the Raritan, in the village cemetery; but those hands are stretched out towards me to-day, and they are just as warm and they are just as gentle as when I sat on her knee at five years of age. And I shall never shake off those hands. I do not want to. They have helped me so much a thousand times already, and I do not expect to have a trouble or a trial between this and my grave where those hands will not help me. It was not a very splendid home, as the world calls it; but we had a family bible there, well worn by tender perusal; and there was a family altar there, where we knelt morning and night; and there was a holy Sabbath there; and stretched in a straight line or hung in loops or festoons there was a scarlet line in the window. O, the tender, precious, blessed memory of a Christian home! Is that the impression you are making upon your children? When you are dead—and it will not be long before you are—when you are dead, will your child say: "If there ever was a good Christian father, mine was one. If there ever was a good Christian mother, mine was one?"

Still further: We want this scarlet line of the text drawn across the window of our prospects. I see Rahab and father, and her mother, and her brothers, and her sisters looking out over Jericho, the city of palm-trees, and across the river, and over at the army invading, and then up to the mountains and the sky. Mind you, this house was on the wall, and I suppose the prospect from the window must have been very wide. Besides that, I do not think that the scarlet line at all interfered with the view of the landscape. The assurance it gave of safety must have added to the beauty of the country. To-day, my friends, we sit in the window of earthly prospects, and we look off towards the hills of heaven and the landscape of eternal beauty. God has opened the window for us, and we look out. We only get a dim outline of the inhabitants. We now only here and there catch a note of the exquisite harmony.

THE SCARLET LINE AT THE WINDOW.

But blessed be God for this scarlet line in the window. That tells me that the blood of Christ bought that home, for my soul, and I shall go there when my work is done And as I put my hand on that scarlet line, every-thing in the future brightens. My eyesight gets better, and the robes of the victors are more lustrous, and our loved ones who went away some time ago—they do not stand any more with their backs to us, but their faces are this way and their voices drop through this Sabbath air, saying with all tenderness and sweetness, "Come! Come! Come!" And the child that you think of only as buried—why, there she is, and it is May day in heaven; and they gather the amaranth, and they pluck the lilies, and they twist then into a garland for her brow, and she is one of the May queens of heaven. O, do you think they could see our waving to-day?

It is quite a pleasant day, pretty clear and, not many clouds in the sky. I wonder if they can see us from that good land? I think they can. If from this window of earthly prospects we can almost see them, then from their towers of light I think they can fully see us. And so I wave them the glory, and I wave them the joy, and I say: "Have you got through with all your troubles?" And their voices answer: "God hath wiped away all tears from our eyes." I say: "Is it as grand up there as you thought it would be?" And the voice answers: "Eye hath not seen nor ear heard, neither hath it entered into the heart of man, the things which God hath prepared for those that love him" I say: "Do you have any more struggle for bread?" and they answer: "We hunger no more, we thirst no more." And I say: "Have you been out to the cemetery of the golden city?" and they answer: "There is no death here." And I look out through the heavens, and say: "Where do you get your light from nights, and what do you burn in the temple?" and they answer: "There

THE RIVER OF THE WATER OF LIFE.

is no night here, and we have no need of candle or of star." And I say: "What book do you sing out of?" and they answer: "The Hallelujah Chorus." And I say: "In the splendor and magnificence of the city, don't you ever get lost?" and they answer: "The Lamb which is in the midst of the throne leadeth us to living fountains of water." O how near they seem. Their wings—do you not feel them? Their harps—do you not hear them? And all that through the window of our earthly prospects, across which stretcheth the scarlet line. Be that my choice color forever. Is it too glaring for you? Do you like the blue because it reminds you of the sky, or the green because it makes you think of the foliage, or the black because it is in the shadows of the night? I take the scarlet because it shall make me think of the price that was paid for my soul. O the blood! the blood! the blood of the Lamb of God that taketh away the sin of the world.

I see where you are· You are at the cross roads. The next step decides everything. Pause before you take it; but do not pause too long. I hear the blast of the trumpet that wakes the dead. Look out! Look out! For in that day, and in our closing moment on earth, better than any other defense or barricade, however high or broad or stupendous, will be one little, thin, scarlet thread in the window.

www.ingramcontent.com/pod-product-compliance
Lightning Source LLC
Chambersburg PA
CBHW020911230426
43666CB00008B/1410